CHINESE COOKERY
Masterclass

CHINESE
COOKERY
Masterclass

Willy Mark
Foreword by Kenneth Lo

CHARTWELL
BOOKS, INC

A QUARTO BOOK

Published by Chartwell Books Inc.
A Division of Book Sales Inc.
110 Enterprise Avenue
Secaucus, New Jersey 07094

First published 1984
Copyright © Quarto Publishing Limited
ISBN 0 89009-787-9

This book was designed and produced by
Quarto Publishing Limited
32 Kingly Court
London W1

Art Editor Jane Willis
Editor Lydia Darbyshire
Editorial Director Christopher Fagg
Photographer Michael Freeman

Quarto would like to extend special thanks to Kenneth Lo for
his invaluable help and advice.

Typeset by Leaper & Gard Ltd, Bristol
Color origination by Hong Kong Graphic Arts Service Center,
Hong Kong
Printed by Leefung-Asco Printers Limited, Hong Kong

CONTENTS

FOREWORD

The economic and financial boom which Hong Kong has been enjoying since the early Fifties is probably bigger than any other in recorded history and, despite the prospect of a change in sovereignty in 1997, that boom seems set to continue. The phenomenon is a remarkable one. Looking at the skyline of Hong Kong today, and recalling the barren island it was not so long ago, makes one realize the unprecedented scale of Hong Kong's success.

One side-effect of economic growth has been the tremendous boom in Hong Kong's food trade. At mealtimes, day in day out, the visitor to any of Hong Kong's hundreds of restaurants is likely to find it crammed to capacity and beyond — a situation by no means common in the majority of the world's great cities. A large and prosperous Chinese population of discriminating eaters-out has had a dramatic effect on the standard of cuisine, with the result that Hong Kong can now justifiably be considered as one of the top food and culinary centers in the world.

The character of Hong Kong styles in food is largely influenced by its proximity to Canton (the Chinese province of Guangdong), with its emphasis on seafood — of which Hong Kong enjoys a superabundance. As a great crossroads of the Far East, however, Hong Kong is host to the other schools of Chinese cuisine — Pekingese, Shanghai and Sichuan — as well as Malaysian food, all of which contribute to a kaleidoscopic gastronomic experience.

In all the hustle, bustle and din of the food world of Hong Kong, the name of Willy Mark has achieved special prominence. Officially the food and wine consultant to the Hong Kong Tourist Association, he is also a famous gourmet and the proprietor of two restaurants in Taiwan, where the food is said to be more authentically Chinese than in Hong Kong itself.

On my own visits to Hong Kong, I have been told on many occasions that Willy Mark is *the* man to talk to about food in Hong Kong. The usual demands of crowded schedules having prevented our meeting, I was delighted recently to meet Willy Mark in London — where good Chinese food is much thinner on the ground than in Hong Kong — and to have the opportunity of reading the manuscript of *Chinese Cookery Masterclass*. I was immediately struck by certain points in his book which make it distinctly different from the normal run of Chinese cookbooks published by the dozen in the west these days.

One of the first things that I noticed is that Willy Mark and his chefs employ a very light touch in the use of Chinese flavoring ingredients. This seems to reflect the taste of the top tables of Hong Kong, where preferences have moved away from over-spiced foods. In New York, by contrast, only highly spiced dishes, and restaurants branded Sichuan or Hunan, will do. In Hong

Kong, freshness and savoriness are the keynotes, and the emphasis is on the exquisite and exotic.

Much of this, as I have indicated, is the legacy of the Cantonese school, with its seafood dishes and delicately flavoured shrimp and oyster sauces. But I was also interested to note that Willy Mark has made a point of describing the Chiu Chow and Hakka styles which are quite distinct from that of Canton. The Hakkas are the Chinese 'gypsies' who have been wandering down into south China from the north for over a millenium, especially during the Yuan dynasty at the time of the Mongol Empire. Their style of cooking is characterized by the blending of fresh flavors with those of highly seasoned wind-dried and preserved foods, and the extensive use of animal parts and variety meats.

Chiu Chow cooking is strongly influenced by the cuisine of the neighboring province of Fukien (where tea is grown in abundance). The seafood here is consumed to the accompaniment of specially concocted dip-sauces, while small cups of strong tea are drunk as punctuation between courses as the meal progresses.

With these, and his selections from the better known Chinese schools, Willy Mark presents an intriguing picture of the innovations which Hong Kong cooking is bringing to Chinese food as a whole. I think it is not too much to say that in China itself cooking has been fairly stagnant for the past three or four decades, and it is taking a great effort on the part of the Chinese government to restore it even to its past glories, let alone to break new ground. In Hong Kong, on the other hand, with its prosperity and close contacts with the west, a 'sea-change' has been imperceptibly taking place over the last decade or two. Some western approaches have been accepted into Chinese cooking which, being so old and confident and massive, has no qualms in accepting anything it regards as useful and interesting. It seems to me that the innovations of Hong Kong Chinese cooking bear the same relationship to traditional Chinese cuisine as does the Nouvelle Cuisine to traditional French cooking — an approach characterized by smaller, lighter dishes that are exquisite in flavor, texture and presentation. In my view, these changes are all to the good, if only because the traditional recipes of the Chinese banquet can often be over-rich and heavy while traditional 'delicacies' — such as bear's paw, elephant trunks, sea slugs and so on — have become unacceptable to contemporary taste.

With these thoughts and impressions in mind, I can thoroughly recommend the reader to delve directly into the book to make his or her own explorations, which will reveal fresh angles of gastronomic interest not easily to be found in other cookbooks.

Kenneth Lo, 1984

INTRODUCTION

COMBINATION CHIU CHOW STARTERS Freshness of ingredients and elegance of presentation are emphasized in these delicious *hors d'oeuvres* from the Southern School of Chinese cuisine.

'Food and love of beauty are in our natures.' Such a Chinese proverb might be found in a fortune cookie for there are truly hundreds of Chinese proverbs about food. In a *real* Chinese restaurant, of course, you would never find a fortune cookie. That abomination of modern marketing techniques is a commercial triumph of the overseas Chinese, just like *chop-suey* — neither has got anything to do with the reality of ancient Chinese cuisine.

'Chinese cuisine' can be a daunting phrase. It is as comprehensive and overwhelming as any label that is attached to a massive portion of mankind's cultural history. 'Chinese cuisine' is as broad a description as 'western civilization'. No one volume could claim to teach a student the whole of western civilization in a couple of hundred illustrated pages, and this book cannot hope to cover the whole of Chinese cuisine. We can give only a sample, some hints and enough recipes to allow the reader to make a culinary voyage of discovery.

'On a journey do not measure the distance', says another ancient proverb. 'And during a meal do not work out the quantity', it continues, with the poetic sense of balance beloved by the Chinese. Some indications of distance and quantity are needed, however, before a stranger ventures into Chinese cooking.

China is a land of 9½ million square kilometres (almost 4 million square miles), whose 1,000 million inhabitants share a history and cultural traditions that stretch back five thousand years. Thus 'Chinese' cooking is in many ways as meaningless a concept as 'European' cooking. China must be divided up if it is to be conquered in a culinary sense.

There are four major schools of Chinese cookery — Peking, Sichuan, Shanghai and Cantonese. Yet again, as we will see, the labels are very broad, and each of the four major regional cooking styles proudly includes individual regional or local variations and specialities.

A map of China will allow us to look at the four major styles on a geographical basis. Peking is the northern region, a vast expanse stretching from the Yellow Sea (facing Korea in the east) to below the Great Wall of China to the south and Inner Mongolia in the west and north.

Sichuan (or Szechuan in its older, Romanized spelling) is the name given to the cooking styles of the western provinces. These lie to the east and south of Sichuan Province itself, from Hankow in Hupei Province to Yunnan Province, which borders on Burma, Thailand and Vietnam.

Shanghai covers the eastern region. The East China Sea washes the shores of Kiangsu, Chekiang and Fukien Provinces, and receives the waters of the great Yangtze River. Shanghai itself, part of the Yangtze delta, is but one of many urban civilizations that created 'Shanghai cuisine'.

Similarly Canton (now called Guangzhou) is merely the major

COOKERY SCHOOLS

Northern/Peking

Peking

Shandong

Eastern/Shanghai

Shanghai

Huaiyang

Suzhe

Hangzhou

Fukien

Western/ Sichuan

Sichuan

Southern/Canton

Guangzhou (Canton)

Dong Jiang

Shantou

city of the southern Chinese school of cooking, which is found in the provinces bordering the South China Sea, and includes Hainan Island, as well as Hong Kong and Macau. Despite their western trappings, both Hong Kong and Macau are fundamentally Cantonese. Some of their special features will be mentioned later, for it is Hong Kong that has produced the environment in which all schools of Chinese cooking have been able to flourish.

Before considering the different attributes and styles of the four major regional schools of cooking, it is important to look at the historical and cultural factors that link all the schools and unite the whole Chinese nation in its love of food.

When a stranger thinks of Chinese food he thinks of *woks* and chopsticks and of convivial shared meals. But why should the Chinese have developed such a particular style of cooking and eating?

It could be claimed that necessity has certainly been the mother of invention as far as the Chinese are concerned. What we know today as Chinese cuisine is often the ancient response to economic adversities. Another Chinese proverb tells us that 'Whatever will satisfy hunger is good food'.

THIS CULINARY MAP of China gives a vivid impression of the sheer scale and variety of the country, from the harsh continental climate of the north to the subtropical regions of the south. With such a range of climates and geography, it is hard to talk in general terms about Chinese cooking. There are no formal divisions between the great schools of Peking (north), Shanghai (east), Canton (south) or Sichuan (west), but rather shifts of emphasis and perspective.

9

MONGOLIAN HOTPOT is a Chinese version of the fondue, with everyone dipping into a rich stock.

The Chinese soon learned the value of that universal truth, waste not, want not, and for me the classic example of this is the world-famous Peking Duck, which is the basis of an entire meal. Even though it could be afforded only by rich diners in the past, it was still a golden example of Chinese cooks' cost-effectiveness and Chinese diners' culinary common sense.

First, the carved duck skin is eaten. Then the skinned bird is taken back to the kitchen for its meat to become a stir-fried second course. Meanwhile the bones are being cooked with vegetables in a soup. A fourth course might be a dish of scrambled eggs cooked in the fat collected during the original roasting. Then there are the duck's variety meats (liver, tongue, etc), and any Chinese cook, from Peking or anywhere, will put aside the feet for other uses. Needless to say, the feathers will already have been sold for non-culinary purposes!

The Chinese *had* to be cost-conscious. The nation has always had to cope with population pressures — even emigration was not a solution — and demand for food always exceeded supply. The Chinese survived in conditions that existed long before Malthus formulated his theories. How?

The answer was to share what little they had in ways that gave each member of a family either a fair share or a shared taste of something special. (However, it must be admitted that even in ancient Chinese communities the women were expected to defer to the males of the family. The head of a fish — the most nutritious part according to ancient beliefs — is still always presented to the head of the household or to the guest of honour so that he may pick out the protein-rich eyes.)

Most of the time a Chinese family might have only a few grams of meat to grace its table. It was socially sensible to shred, dice or mince it, blending it with the more plentiful roots or vegetables so that everyone could share it. If the meat supply was too small even for that, it would be carefully transformed into a flavoring for the vegetables.

That's why chopsticks evolved. Known to have been in existence for over three thousand years, they were the ideal invention for a people forced to eat fragments of food. Hands and fingers were outlawed. Some say that chopsticks were invented so that every member of the family could dip into the food on a table without rising from the floor or chairs. Others suggest that hygiene was a major motive. It is more likely that a frugal diet compelled the Chinese to find a device that would limit any one diner's greed.

Chopsticks proved to be brilliant tools in the fingers of experienced operators. In the kitchen they are perfect whisks, tongs and cleavers of soft foods, for versatility was another virtue encouraged by economic necessity. No Chinese family could afford the battalion of specialized cooking utensils other nations lined up in their kitchens.

And that's how the *wok* developed too. As the modern western world has discovered to its joy, a *wok* is a multi-purpose invention. It can cook anything except roast meat. In experienced hands it can even cook more than one dish at a time, with a metal stand and a lid to cover the double-cooker.

In the north, where fewer inhabitants meant greater access to meat supplies, the Mongolian hot pots or fire pots still encouraged group dining. A family would gather around the cooking pot, dipping the thinly sliced meats into a 'moat' of stock bubbling around a central chimney. Comparable in some ways to western fondue cooking, Mongolian hot pots are one aspect of 'Peking' food.

FOR THE CHINESE, eating is always a shared experience.

The deep sense of family is therefore both a cause and effect of Chinese cooking conventions. The Chinese family did not stay together because it prayed together (temple prayers being women's work); it stayed together, as one terrible punster put it, because it played chopsticks together.

Nevertheless there *is* an abiding love of food among all Chinese. It verges on worship. The ways that ingredients are chosen, prepared, cooked and balanced are, effectively, a constant way of 'saying grace', of offering thanks to the gods. The Kitchen God or God of the Hearth is one of the most important to a family. Every

Chinese New Year the Kitchen God returns to heaven to report to the Jade Emperor on the family's behavior during the year just ended. To ensure that the report is favorable, housewives undertake an enormous spring-cleaning operation. Cracked and damaged crockery or utensils are replaced, and a Chinese kitchen, always scrupulously clean, becomes even more spotless. The Kitchen God must also be given a good meal before he flies off for his annual visit to heaven. Glutinous rice and fruits, horse hay, sugar and bean curd are offered, while the family itself celebrates with a better-than-everyday meal. As with most temple or shrine food offerings, waste is avoided: the humans will consume the offerings once the satisfied God has flown off.

The Kitchen God returns to the family on the fourth day of the New Year, the day when married women are expected to visit their parents, thus giving some housewives at least a break from their own kitchens!

Almost every Chinese dish has superstitious or symbolic attributes. Sometimes the auspicious quality of a dish will come from an ingredient's name. At other times an ingredient's supposed restorative or aphrodisiac qualities are honored. Other dishes, such as the Mid-Autumn Festival moon cakes, recall historical or mythological events.

A whole library could be filled with books about Chinese culinary symbols. To give just one example associated with New Year dining, consider the purple-black sea moss strands that are a favored part of every Spring Festival dinner. The Cantonese call it *fat choi* (*choi* being the standard character for every vegetable), and its name is remarkably close to part of the standard New Year greeting of *Kung Hei Fat Choy,* which wishes everyone good fortune and prosperity for the New Year. So *fat choi* is a treasured ingredient.

Above all else the concept of balance is crucial in appreciating — and cooking — Chinese cuisine. The concept, akin to Confucianism's middle way, is the very basis of Chinese society and beliefs. A human can acquire a state of equilibrium only if he or she ensures that the Yin (negative) and Yang (positive) forces are in balance. There are three other pairs of potential lines of tension: cold and hot; empty and full; and outer and inner.

Thus the Chinese believe that 'we are what we eat' and that 'we eat to reinforce'. Food is the best medicine. A well-balanced diet, even among the poorest families, will guarantee good health, for the food itself will contain all the goodness a man needs if it is prepared and cooked properly, eaten in its right season and not allowed to clash with antagonistic foods. If antagonisms have been set up through ignorance, a herbalist will prescribe the appropriate natural cure.

Western dieticians have confirmed the ancient wisdoms of Chinese cooking guides and herbalists' instruction manuals. The most famous cure-all, and an expensive sexual restorative for ageing men, is ginseng, the mermaid-shaped root herb, which is recommended as a treatment for asthma, anaemia, headaches, nausea, rheumatism, heart disease and even indigestion. Indeed, I remember in my home province seeing treasured ginseng roots kept ready by elderly rich men. When they knew they had entered their last days, they would summon their far-off sons and consume the gingseng in soup form. The soup was believed power-

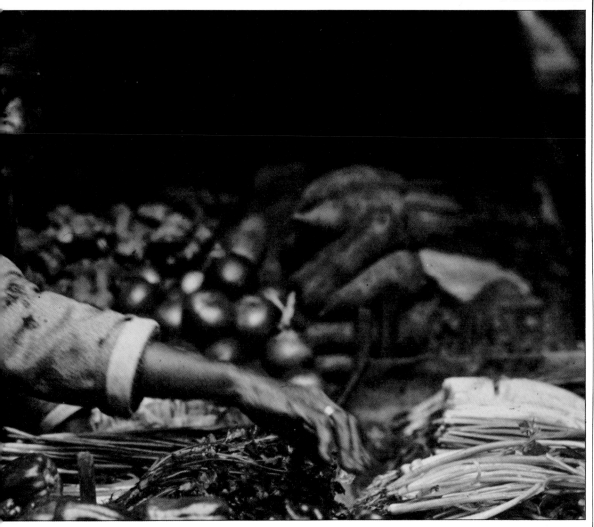

ful enough to keep them alive until their sons arrived back home.

Perhaps, as in many folk cures, a food's efficacy depends on belief rather than actual scientific properties. In China I doubt it. The Chinese have been testing their culinary magic for five thousand years, and they know what works.

Ginger and mint strengthen thin blood. 'Cool' foods calm down hot-blooded youngsters. Bird's nests and petals aid a lady seeking skin perfection. Cold Chinese tea dabbed on the skin prevents wrinkles. Chrysanthemum tea is good for the eyes. Snake bile truly fortifies the over-forties . . . the list of health-giving properties in the pantheon of Chinese recipes is endless.

A stranger need not give up in despair. It is not necessary to know the whole culinary pharmacology. Indeed, there are few Chinese cooks who can remember all the factors, myths and rules surrounding their cuisine. Good cooks rely on their senses and on common sense. For all the marvellous aspects of Chinese culinary folklore are really codified common sense. A Chinese cook seeks to achieve balance, in one dish or in a whole banquet, by satisfying the diner's eyes (presentation), his nose (sequence of aromas) and his palate (taste combinations). Once again we must ascribe such perfectionism to poverty. If a family has a frugal diet it must make the best of it, creating appetizing interest and leisurely enjoyment of a dining experience.

A HONG KONG market vegetable stall offers a colorful abundance of vegetables and fresh spices and herbs, including fresh root ginger, coriander and chives.

13

COOKING TECHNIQUES

HEAT CONTROL IS the key to successful Chinese cuisine.

Chinese food is to be found all over the world, and the art of the Chinese kitchen has followers and admirers everywhere. Few of those admirers would deny that the uncontested capital of Chinese gastronomy is Hong Kong, which has become a paradise for lovers of the very best in Chinese food.

Chinese food can be divided in the main into four schools — Peking, Sichuan, Shanghai and Cantonese — and in Hong Kong these different schools have in many cases been improved and enhanced by outstanding chefs who have developed superb cooking techniques.

Over the last two decades, I have had the opportunity to get to know these master-cooks on the countless occasions I have dined out in Hong Kong's best Chinese restaurants. Many of them are now my personal friends, and it is because of this that I have been able to persuade them to disclose their secrets — their use of ingredients, cooking techniques, timing. From my conversations and from the practical information I gleaned, I have been able to compile this book of choice recipes from the most distinguished Chinese master-chefs in Hong Kong. I should like to take this opportunity to thank them all for their generosity and cooperation.

The book should give readers the opportunity to learn the art of Chinese cuisine. Most of the recipes in this book are Cantonese, but there are also some dishes from Peking, Sichuan, Shanghai and Chiu Chow. The cooking methods and recipes have all been tested, and the criterion for selection was that the cooking techniques should be comparatively simple. Readers will find that they can proceed in a step-by-step manner, in easy stages. The amount of seasonings may be easily adjusted according to individual taste, and with practice, heat control will become a matter of habit. Your cooking skills should improve rapidly as you practise, and by trial and error you will learn how to adjust the recipes to your taste.

There are many aspects to Chinese cooking, but if you can master certain basic skills and understand the underlying principles, you will soon be able to cook 'real' Chinese food and produce some truly authentic Chinese dishes.

A number of accepted Chinese cooking methods are used continually, and they can be summarized as boiling (slow-simmering and rapid boiling); steaming; stir-frying; shallow frying; deep frying; braising and stewing. The uses of the kitchen knife can be categorized as chopping, cutting, slicing, shredding and mincing.

Remember: heat control is of paramount importance in Chinese cooking. Dishes have to be cooked at just the right temperature for just the right length of time. Generally speaking, you need to use the highest heat for quick steaming and stir-frying; medium heat for braising, poaching and boiling, and low heat for shallow frying and stewing. For deep frying, the heat should be varied according to the ingredients used and dishes to be produced; it could be high, medium or low and may require variation in the course of the cooking.

SOME COOKING METHODS are swift and spectacular.

Seasonings

There are far too many seasonings to list here, but the most basic category of all are those made from soya beans. All kinds of soy sauce are made from beans, so are bean paste, preserved bean curd and preserved fermented black beans. You will begin to get the authentic Chinese flavor by combining any of the above with garlic, ginger and with scallions. Traditionally, Cantonese chefs enjoy using oyster sauce, and in this book you will see how many of Hong Kong's most famous chefs frequently employ oyster sauce in their recipes.

In my opinion, the following seasonings would be sufficient: sweet soy sauce, soy sauce, oyster sauce, black bean paste, yellow bean paste, sesame oil, rice wine, pepper, sugar, rice vinegar and cornstarch. Most ordinary Chinese dishes can be prepared using any of the above in combination with garlic, ginger and with scallions, and with dried orange peel. If your tastes incline you to be even more demanding, you may add fermented black beans, Chu How sauce, shrimp sauce, seafood sauce, Chinese prickly ash, star anise, mandarin peel, cloves, aniseed, fennel, dried chilies and a bottle of brine.

Equipment

To get the best results, you do need the traditional round-bottom Chinese pan, the *wok*. You can use it successfully for any cooking method mentioned so far, especially for stir-frying.

As far as the kind of stove you use is concerned, you will not be able to get such good results with an electric stove, which does not give the instant heat control or the space between the *wok* and the heat that enables the flame to caress the bottom of the *wok* and spread the heat evenly. Apart from that problem, you

THE CHINESE *batterie de cuisine* is minimal.

can successfully use gas, kerosene or bottled gas for Chinese cooking and get good results with any of them.

Cooking temperatures
The temperature of the cooking oil will also have to be varied according to the ingredients used and the dishes to be produced.

Hot pan with cold oil Heat the pan until very hot, then add the cold oil. Put in the ingredients before the oil gets really hot and remove the ingredients after deep frying for a short time. This method requires the temperature of the oil to be 175-210°F. When you add the ingredients, there should be no smoke from the oil and no hissing sound. This method is used to prepare good cuts of meat as it helps to retain their natural flavor and preserves the tenderness of the meat.

Hot pan with hot oil Heat the pan until very hot, then add the oil and heat it to a temperature of 350-425°F. The oil should start to smoke, and it will hiss if you stir it. This method is used to prepare seafood and food that requires a crunchy covering (often battered foods).

Medium heat with hot oil Heat the pan until very hot, then heat the oil until it reaches a temperature of 225-330°F. A small amount of smoke will begin to come off the surface of the oil. This method is used for frying large pieces of meat, whole fish, chicken or duck.

Stir-frying
The ability to stir-fry is an important part of any Cantonese chef's skill. It is essential to heat the pan over maximum gas or electricity until it is extremely hot. Then add the necessary quantity of oil. When that is hot, add minced or chopped garlic, ginger and scallion. As the mixture begins to cook, add all the other ingredients, then stir-fry and turn them to cook everything quickly and evenly. Sprinkle wine and sesame oil at the end to produce a fragrant smell.

Chinese shallow frying
For shallow frying, heat the pan until it is extremely hot and then add oil. Lower the ingredient into the pan and, when it is slightly brown, reduce the heat to a minimum. Use this method to fry fish. It will stop the skin sticking to the pan and ensure an attractive appearance when it is served.

Deep frying
This is a popular technique in Chinese cooking. Strictly speaking, blanching the ingredients in oil can be regarded as deep frying. To deep fry you need, in most cases, adequate heat and hot oil to make the ingredients crunchy and tender. Be careful, however, with ingredients that are coated in batter: keep the temperature somewhat lower, otherwise you will overcook the outside of the food while the inside is still raw. In these cases, it might be better to use the 'soak-frying' method. Heat the oil, add the ingredients and turn off the heat. Let them soak for a while in the hot oil and then take them out. Reheat the oil until it reaches a temperature of 350-425°F and then deep fry the ingredients for a second time, until done. This cooking method is also known as double deep frying.

Steaming

There are two kinds of steaming. Short steaming, requiring high heat, and long steaming, requiring low heat. Some other Chinese cook books may call long steaming 'double boiling' because the foods are contained in a closed receptacle. In some recipes, those calling for the steaming of a duck, chicken or a large piece of meat for example, you should use the low, medium heat until the ingredients are tender.

Boiling

This is a very simple method of cooking. Simply add water to cook the ingredients, exactly as you would cook soup, rice or porridge. If you want to make a bowl of clear meat soup, you must blanch the meat with boiling water first, and then rinse it under cold water. Heat a bowlful of water in a pan and, when the water is boiling, put the ingredients into it. You should use maximum heat at the start, reducing to medium heat and finally ending with low heat. This kind of soup is delicious once you have mastered the timing and the amount of water to add.

Braising

Cook ingredients over moderate heat with sufficient liquid to cover them. Reduce the liquid to 15 per cent of the original and add seasonings to make a sauce.

Stewing

Add more water or stock and use low heat to cook the ingredients until they are soft and tender. Once the liquid has nearly all evaporated — or reduced to 10-20 per cent — add seasonings, ingredients and flavoring to make the sauce.

Use of knife or cleaver

The ingredients in Chinese cooking are frequently prepared by using a knife or sharp cleaver. Many recipes are prepared by the 'cut-and-cook' method, which requires that equal attention is paid to both the cutting and the cooking. Whether you are preparing ingredients by cutting them into chunky pieces, or by slicing, thick shredding, fine shredding, dicing into cubes or mincing, you must always ensure that everything is of equal size. If you do not, then the quality of the cooking will be affected because of the uneven heating which will result.

There is a Chinese saying: 'If we want to do our jobs properly, we must first sharpen our tools.' To do your kitchen work properly, you need a good sharp cleaver and a heavy chopping-board. Any good quality Chinese chopper will be more than adequate, and a traditional thick chopping-board made of solid wood, approximately 5-6in thick, is much better than the skimpy modern ones. Many westerners are afraid of using a razor-sharp Chinese kitchen chopper. The secret for beginners is to avoid cutting horizontally. Instead, use your whole hand on the top of the blade, rather than chopping from the handle, and slice carefully into the ingredients at an angle. This is risk-free and easy, thanks to the sharpness of the blade.

Slicing

This is the most usual form of cutting. Slicing meat across the grain makes it more tender when cooked: slices should be little thicker than cardboard.

Meat is sliced across the grain.

The thickness of vegetable slices depends on their texture.

Shredding

Ingredients are cut into thin slices then shredded into fine strips.

Meat is shredded into matchstick-thin strips.

Shredding bamboo shoots.

Dicing

Ingredients are cut into coarse strips then diced into small cubes.

Chicken breast is cut into strips.

The strips are cut horizontally into small cubes.

Chopping

The Chinese cleaver is ideal for jointing and chopping fish or fowl into the bite-sized pieces the Chinese love. This sequence illustrates how to joint and chop chicken.

1 Remove the wings.

2 Remove the legs and thighs.

3 Cut the breast away from the backbone.

4 Divide the breast in two.

5 Cut each breast into three or four pieces.

6 Cut wings into three pieces and legs into five pieces. Now reassemble the bird neatly.

Pork slices are first shredded.

Chopping becomes progressively finer.

Grinding (mincing)

Grinding is usually done by hand. A mincer can also be used — but some of the flavor will be lost.

Carrots are cut on the diagonal.

Pepper strips are cut into diamond shapes.

Diagonal cutting

This is the usual technique for chopping vegetable such as celery, carrots and zucchini.

Remove the large bone.

Chop the separated ribs into small pieces.

Preparing pork spare ribs

This method of preparation makes the spare ribs easy to eat.

THE CHEFS

NG CHI FUNG
Master of Peking cuisine

Ng Chi Fung is one of the outstanding Peking cuisine chefs in Hong Kong. Born in Chiu Chou, he is now the chef de cuisine of Hong Kong's King Heung Restaurant. He began his career in 1958 when he joined Hou Tak Food Restaurant and learned cooking from the famous northern master cooks known as the Four Aces, who were in charge of the kitchen at that time. Today he, too, is a master of Peking cuisine.

For Ng Chi Fung, experience is the decisive factor in Chinese cooking skills. A sharp eye and quick reflexes are essential — and can be developed only through many years' training.

HO SING
Chef de cuisine of one of the world's top ten restaurants

Ho Sing is the chef de cuisine of Yung Kee, designated by *Fortune* magazine as one of the ten best restaurants in the world. Universally known to Hong Kong eaters-out as 'Seventh Uncle', Mr Ho started to learn to cook in restaurants in Central District, Hong Kong, at the age of nine. During the World War II, he ran his own restaurant in Canton but returned to Hong Kong after the war and has been in his present position as the Kitchen Master since 1970. Like all first-rate chefs, Mr Ho pays special attention to selecting the freshest ingredients and tailoring menus to the individual occasion. The element of harmony is of the greatest importance in Mr Ho's approach, whether it is the aesthetic harmony of tastes, flavors and aromas or the practical coordination of prepared ingredients and cooking temperatures.

LEUNG KING
Hong Kong's Number One chef

Mr Leung King has reigned supreme as the premier chef of Hong Kong for longer than most people can remember. Now 72, he has been working in the kitchen for 60 years. When he was the chief chef of Lok Yu Tea House, knowledgeable customers insisted that their dishes were prepared personally by him. He is particularly famous for preparing the game recipes and 'Phoenix City Style' cuisine, which many people think of as the cream of Cantonese cooking. I have been fortunate enough to know 'Uncle King' for many years, and his advice has been invaluable in preparing this book.

CHAN WING YUEN
Master of Sichuan cuisine

Not many chefs working in Sichuan restaurants are themselves originally from the province itself. Chan Wing Yuen is one of the exceptions. Born in Chung King City, Sichuan, he is now the chef de cuisine at the Cleveland Sichuan Restaurant. From the age of 16 he started cooking under his father's direction, and he later worked with many famous chefs to improve his techniques.

Chan Wing Yuen has tried to preserve the style of traditional Sichuan Cuisine while at the same time exploring the possibility of using new ingredients. He points out that many people identify Sichuan cuisine only with hot spicy food — but in fact, the balance of seasonings in the preparation of Sichuan cuisine is very complex. The characteristic Sichuan seasonings and methods should combine with mellow color, fragrant smell and taste to make a deliciously balanced ensemble.

HO PAK
King of Young Pigeon

Ho Pak is the principal chef of the Lung Wah Hotel — famous throughout the world for its succulent roast pigeon dishes. Mr Ho did not begin to learn cooking until he was 37, when he started at the Lung Wah. His most famous recipes are young pigeon in soy sauce and young pigeon baked in salt.

LEE BUN
Master of Shark's Fin cookery

Lee Bun is the chief chef of Sin Tung Lok Shark's Fins Restaurant at the Harbour City. Now 36, he joined the profession at the age of 16. In 20 years of cooking experience he has studied under famous masters of cooking, and specializes in cooking shark's fin, abalone, sea food and game. Mr Lee is famous for the care he brings to selecting ingredients for freshness and quality.

LEUNG KUNG
Versatile master of Chinese cuisine

Leung Kung is the principal chef for Chinese cuisine at the Food Street chain of restaurants. At 52, he has 37 years of cooking experience. Having undergone a traditional training under famous cooking masters, he believes that the mastery of the Chinese chef is expressed in an effortless, instinctive control, born of long experience, in blending ingredients, seasoning and cooking temperature to produce food at its very best. Mr Leung defines his own approach to cooking as 'open-mindedness and objectivity'. The range of cuisines offered by the Food Street chain is ample evidence of the breadth of his interests and his willingness to learn.

SOUTHERN SCHOOL

GEESE FLOCKS on a southern farm.

It is Cantonese cooking that most people think of when they think of Chinese food. Waves of emigration from the city and countryside of Guangdong, formerly known as Kwongtung, Province from the mid-nineteenth century onwards established the Cantonese as the major portion of the world's overseas Chinese population. The Fukienese emigrated to the Philippines, the Hoklo to Singapore, but the Cantonese went further afield in search of their family fortunes.

They left China, for London or Hawaii, for the goldfields of Australia, California or Canada, or for wherever a boat could take them, for economic reasons. Although Guangdong Province was naturally fairly fertile and favored with fish and cereals, the peasant's life in some less blessed areas was hard. The Cantonese emigrants worked hard and they saved hard to send money home to support their families and add an ancestral home to their clan villages. When the goldfields ran out or when the railway tracks reached the end of their lines, the Cantonese workers stayed on. Social and economic pressures often restricted them to three activities in which they could be independent: laundries, market gardens and restaurants.

All three interests echoed Cantonese ways of life. Cleanliness is indeed next to godliness for a Cantonese mother, and freshness is a fetish with some Cantonese cooks, who will go to the markets twice-daily to ensure that the family food is glisteningly fresh. Climatic reasons largely account for that health-consciousness. Guangdong and the neighbouring province of Guangxi are subtropical, with long spells of humidity. Before refrigerators were available, storing food was not feasible, and the alternative of preserving ingredients rarely appealed to Cantonese tastes.

The Cantonese adherence to ancient Taoist ideas about the scientific and systematic uses of food further accounts for that passion for freshness. The Cantonese believe that, on the whole, ingredients should be changed as little as possible during cooking. Cooking methods should therefore be as simple, straightforward and brief as possible. Vegetables are stir-fried and fish steamed to keep them as near to their natural state as possible, consistent with the dishes being made appetizing. In common with other Chinese however, the Cantonese do not eat much that is raw; steak tartare, pink lamb and *sashimi* have taken a long time to find appreciative palates in Hong Kong.

If raw food is unacceptable so is food that has been overcooked. 'Double boiled' soups and 'long simmered' dishes are exceptions in the Cantonese kitchen: food should be braised or stewed briefly, for only a few minutes, which, of course, brings this ancient Chinese style of cooking into line with modern theories of nutrition.

After cleanliness and freshness, the Taoist-influenced Cantonese placed great faith in vegetables. Vegetable cultivation was a major activity between the twice-annual rice harvests, the vegetable plots filling the gaps in a family's or village's plots of land. Even now, the small territory of Hong Kong, a land-hungry enclave, manages to produce a large proportion of its own fresh vegetables. A Hong Kong Cantonese cook may depend on China for running water, pork, chickens, ducks and most of his rice, but he can find his staple vegetables in local markets.

In line with Taoist beliefs, the Cantonese old wives' tales advise which vegetable to eat or cook with which meat or fish, when and why. Each vegetable has its season and its special attributes. Wrong contrasts are reputed to cause digestive disasters. Excesses of any particular vegetable or root have dire consequences, from cramps while you are swimming to insomnia.

Raised on detailed analyses of food, a Cantonese child nearly always became a knowledgeable gourmet, for his region's cuisine has great scope. Guangdong Province has a kindly climate, plenty of water and fertile ground. Versatility was encouraged. The Cantonese consequently have been more ingenious, innovative and inventive when it comes to food than any other Chinese. As we have seen, economic necessity compelled the Cantonese to be catholic in their tastes, but whether that or their natural love of dabbling in the kitchen arts came first is debatable. All we may say for sure is that Cantonese cooks are the best.

CANTONESE CHEFS take pride in presenting food beautifully.

An old Chinese saying claims that an ideal life would be achieved if one were born in Suzhou (famed for its beautiful women), got dressed in Hangzhou (famed for fine silks), died in Luzhou (where the best coffin wood is found) but ate in Guangzhou (Canton). There is truth in this poetic balance.

The inhabitants of Guangdong and Guangxi were independent characters. Only partially absorbed into the Han empire during the Chin dynasty (a little over 2,000 years ago), the Cantonese, like other southerners, have kept their own dialect and culinary traditions. They are particularly proud of their culinary imaginativeness. A Cantonese saying asserts that anything that walks, swims, crawls or flies with its back to Heaven is edible.

Adaptability is another feature of the Cantonese. Two of the region's best-known dishes illustrate this. Sweet-and-sour pork and *chop-suey* — many a Westerner's idea of typical Chinese food (together with fried rice) — are recent Cantonese inventions. Designed to satisfy the tastes of 'red-haired barbarians', the dishes are, ironically, 'typically' Cantonese.

The taste contrasts in sweet-and-sour pork are a favorite Cantonese cooking ploy, the use of one flavor highlighting another. However, the dish was supposedly invented in Guangzhou (Canton city), for centuries a port open to foreign influences ever since Arab traders arrived fifteen centuries ago.

The Mandarins from northern China were also considered foreigners. The Hans brought their own house-chefs when they set up offices in the south, and that led to the further broadening of Cantonese recipes and the development of skilled Cantonese 'Pekinese' cooks. When Europeans settled in Guangzhou to pursue their own trade interests directly, rather than through Arab middlemen, outside influences further expanded Cantonese cuisine. First the Portuguese, then every other nation had its colony of traders dealing in silk, tea, porcelain, spices and other products. Most of them loved sweet-and-sour dishes.

Meanwhile, in nineteenth-century Guangzhou, the development of a true Cantonese cuisine was being pushed to a new peak by the city's wealthy class. Salt merchants and the tycoons of the thirteen *hongs* (agents) of foreign traders encouraged their cooks to outrival each other, and, as in Imperial Peking, an age of ostentatiously grand dining dawned.

The Cantonese had always believed in eating anything. Their love of frog legs, turtles, dogs, snakes and many kinds of exotic species was greater than that of other Chinese. Wealth allowed the merchant class to discover new, costly ingredients, or to persevere until their cooks had worked out the proper cooking methods for each ingredient. The expensive shark's fin and bird's nest dishes were perfected by the Cantonese and their cousins, the Chiu Chow people.

FRESH BEAN CURD on a Hong Kong market stall.

Before we turn to Chiu Chow territory we must not forget Guangdong Province's greatest contribution to Chinese cuisine — *dimsum*, those tasty little snacks that are ideal for taking with tea and were, indeed, virtually invented as a tea-shop cuisine. The Chinese characters of the word indicate their purpose — 'touch the heart' — and show that *dimsum* are a Cantonese passion.

There are possibly 2,000 different varieties of *dimsum*, for the Cantonese prefer to have a number of small meals each day rather than a few large ones (just as Filipinos take *merienda* snacks all day long). A Cantonese day starts with morning tea (*yum cha*) and a *dimsum* breakfast. The delicate *dimsum* concoctions are generally steamed by well-paid specialist cooks who are a law unto themselves. Rarely made at home, *dimsum* are a fine excuse for eating out — from dawn to dusk in Hong Kong — and the average *dimsum* restaurant will offer at least sixty varieties, depending on the season and market supplies.

The tea-drinking habits of the Chiu Chow illustrate how different they are from the Cantonese. The Chiu Chow people originate from the area around the seaport of Swatow in the east of Guangdong Province. Being so close to the Fukien border, it is not surprising that strong Fukienese influences are found in Chiu Chow cuisine. The special Chiu Chow tea is a very good example. Probably China's strongest, bitterest tea, the 'Iron Buddha' tea from Fukien is sipped out of thimble-sized cups. Two cups for each diner before a meal prepare the digestive juices for the heartiness of Chiu Chow food; two cups each after a meal settle the digestion.

As Chiu Chow is by the sea, seafood features largely on the menu, with special recipes for fish, prawn, crabs, oysters and clams. Chiu Chow people put great emphasis on sauces and flavorings to accompany their food, using garlic-vinegar sauce as a dip for spicy goose, while broad bean paste accompanies fish and tangerine jam flatters steamed lobsters.

The third major subdivision within Cantonese cuisine is that of the Hakka people. They are of northern Chinese origin who, having migrated south, mainly settled in Guangdong and Fukien, acquiring the name Hakka (or 'guest family') from the southerners. The thirteenth-century Mongol invasion is said to have prompted their wandering. Because they had been wandering for so long, their cuisine had become one that featured simple dishes and preserved ingredients.

Hakka cuisine is basically poorer than those of the Cantonese and Chiu Chow. It is considered to have the strongest flavors of all, and it includes dishes like salt-roasted chicken, stuffed bean curd, fried beef balls with vegetables and other simple recipes. It is similar to the others in its preference for contrasted, natural flavors and its willingness to cook anything and any part of a carcass. That was a natural trait for a wandering people, and one that is shared by the 'sea gypsies' of the east coast, such as the Hoklo. As in their food and that of the Chiu Chow, Fukienese influences merge with those of Guangdong.

Hong Kong is the birthplace of the third stage of the development of Cantonese cuisine. Lobster salad, Chinese vegetables in Portuguese sauce, baked stuffed conch and the various 'sizzling' styled Chinese dishes are typical examples of the creativity of Hong Kong chefs in presenting Chinese food in western culinary styles. Even restaurant service styles have been westernized, and an almost French-style elegance is now common in top restaurants. Soups will be ladled out, main dishes spooned out individually and all dishes presented on silver platters. However, Hong Kong restaurants have never tried to introduce fortune cookies. The proximity to Guangzhou has kept Hong Kong Cantonese food authentic, while the knowledge of western culinary practices has inspired Hong Kong Cantonese cooks to experiment in ways that have added a new finesse to their classic repertoires.

GUANGDONG PROVINCE has an agreeable climate, fertile soil and plenty of water, which make it ideal for farming. Here a Hakka woman, in traditional dress, tends cattle.

27

PEPPERY SHRIMP

1½lb shrimp
2 cups peanut oil
2 tsp salt
½ tsp sugar

1 tsp chopped garlic
1 tsp minced red chili
1 tsp Chinese yellow wine

Trim and devein the shrimp but leave the shells on. Pat them dry and set aside.

Heat the peanut oil in a pan and add the shrimp to fry for 2 minutes. Turn off the heat and let them sit in the oil for another 2 minutes. Drain and set aside.

Reheat the pan and add the salt, stirring over a low heat until it is slightly browned. Transfer the salt to a saucer and mix with ½ tsp sugar. Set aside.

Heat 1 tbsp oil in pan. Add the garlic and chili and return the shrimp. Stir-fry them over a high heat for 1 minute and add the Chinese yellow wine, stirring for 20 seconds. Sprinkle the salt and sugar mixture over the shrimp, stir-fry for a further 30 seconds and serve.

This is a deliciously hot and spicy Cantonese dish — which is also the restaurant chef's trade secret to disguise shrimps no longer in prime condition!

CREAM OF SWEET CORN AND FISH SOUP

8oz fillet of cod or any white fish

Seasoning
1 tsp salt
½ tsp sesame oil
½ tsp pepper
1 tsp cornstarch

1 cup water

2 cups chicken stock
8oz canned cream of sweet corn
1 tbsp cornstarch
2 eggs
1 tbsp chopped fresh coriander
  (cilantro)

Garnish
2 tbsp finely chopped ham

Dice the fillet of fish into small pieces and mix well with the seasoning ingredients. Set aside.

Boil the water and add the seasoned fish, removing the fish from the water when it starts to boil again. Set aside.

Heat the chicken stock in a pan and stir in the cream of sweet corn. Mix the cornstarch with 1 tbsp of water and add to the sweet corn mixture. Beat the eggs and add them to the mixture with the diced fish and chopped coriander.

Garnish with finely chopped ham.

夏
令
小
炒

STIR-FRIED SHRIMP AND CHICKEN WITH ONION, CUCUMBER AND FRESH MUSHROOMS

9-11oz chicken breasts
3 tsp cornstarch
3 tsp salt
$\frac{1}{4}$ tsp pepper
1 tsp sesame oil
11oz shrimp, shelled and deveined
1 egg white
1 medium onion
12oz cucumber
8oz fresh button mushrooms
2 cups boiling water (for blanching
    mushrooms)
2 cups peanut oil

2 tsp chopped ginger
2 tsp chopped garlic

Sauce
1 tbsp oyster sauce
1 tbsp light soy sauce
1 tsp dark soy sauce
1 tsp sesame oil
1 tsp sugar
8 tbsp chicken stock
1 tbsp cornstarch
1 tsp Chinese yellow wine

Cut the chicken breasts into slices. Marinate the slices in a mixture of 1 tsp cornstarch, $\frac{1}{2}$ tsp salt, $\frac{1}{4}$ tsp pepper and 1 tsp sesame oil. Set to one side.

Clean the shrimp, pat them dry and mix them with 1 egg white, 2 tsp cornstarch and $\frac{1}{2}$ tsp salt. Refrigerate them for 1 hour.

Cut the onion into wedges and separate the pieces, and cut the cucumber into $\frac{1}{2}$in slices.

Halve the fresh mushrooms and blanch them in boiling water with 2 tsp salt added for $1\frac{1}{2}$ minutes. Remove from the water and drain well.

Heat the oil in a pan until hot and add the shrimp, stirring to separate them. As soon as their color changes, take them out of the pan. Drain and set aside.

Turn off the heat and add the chicken, again stirring to separate. Remove when the color changes (in $1\frac{1}{2}$ minutes). Drain and set aside.

Heat 1 tbsp oil in the pan. Add the onion, stir and cook until soft. Transfer to a plate.

Heat 1 tbsp oil in the pan, adding 1 tsp ginger and 1 tsp garlic. When the aroma arises, add the fresh mushrooms, stir and cook for 30 seconds. Add the cucumber slices, stir and cook for 30 seconds. Transfer to a plate.

Heat 2 tbsp oil in the pan. Add the remaining chopped ginger and garlic and, when the aroma arises, add the shrimp and chicken. Stir and cook for 1 minute over a medium heat. Return the onion, cucumber and mushrooms to the pan. Mix the sauce ingredients and add to the pan, stirring rapidly over a very high heat for 45 seconds. Serve.

If you prefer to have more sauce, simply double the quantity of the ingredients. This dish is good when it is served with plain cooked rice.

粟米魚茸羹

PEPPERY SHRIMP
A spicy version of a popular Cantonese dish which makes an excellent starting point for the beginner in Chinese cuisine. The cuisine of Canton (Guangdong) Province, with its emphasis on seafood, is the foundation of Hong Kong style cooking

CREAM OF SWEET CORN AND FISH SOUP
A simple dish with very full flavor brought out by the addition of coriander, which also serves a decorative purpose.

STEAMED SHRIMP WITH SCALLIONS AND LIGHT SOY SAUCE

2lb shrimp (3-4in)
5 cups boiling water
4 tbsp peanut oil
2 tbsp chopped scallions
2 garlic cloves

Sauce
2 tbsp light soy sauce
2 tsp Chinese yellow wine
4 tbsp chicken stock

Slit the shrimp open along the back and devein them. Clean and pat them dry and arrange them neatly on a plate.

Bring the water to the boil in a wok with a rack in it. Place the plate on the rack and cover the wok. Steam the shrimp over a high heat for 5-7 minutes. Remove the plate from the wok and drain all accumulated liquid away from the shrimp. Sprinkle chopped scallions over the shrimp and set aside.

Heat the oil in a pan and add the crushed garlic. When the garlic turns brown, drain off the excess oil.

Blend the sauce ingredients and add them to the pan. When the sauce is hot, pour it over the shrimp and serve.

THREE DELICACIES STUFFED WITH SHRIMP

1 eggplant
4 green peppers
4 tomatoes
$\frac{1}{4}$ cup pork fat
12oz fresh shelled shrimp

Seasonings
1 egg white
1 tsp cornstarch
$\frac{1}{2}$ tsp salt
$\frac{1}{4}$ tsp peppers

few drops of sesame oil

2 tbsp cornstarch
2 tbsp peanut oil

Sauce
1 tbsp tomato juice
2 tsp catsup
2 tsp soy sauce
5 tbsp chicken stock
1 tsp sugar

Cut the eggplant into slices $\frac{1}{2}$in thick and cut a slit in each piece.

Cut the green peppers in half and remove the seeds, and cut the tomatoes in half and remove the pulp.

Dice the pork fat finely. Chop and mash the shrimp into a paste, continuing to stir and beat the paste until it becomes sticky. Add the diced pork fat and continue to stir, and then mix the seasonings with the shrimp paste. Refrigerate for 2 hours.

Coat the inside of the eggplant, green peppers and tomatoes with cornstarch and stuff them with the shrimp mixture.

Heat the pan over a high heat. Add 2 tbsp oil and fry the eggplant, green peppers and tomatoes, open side down, over a medium heat for 1½ minutes.

Mix and blend the sauce ingredients in a bowl and pour the mixture evenly over the stuffed vegetables. Cover the pan and cook for 2 more minutes, then serve piping hot.

An exotic variant of this dish uses bitter melon, large red chilies and bean curd instead of tomatoes and eggplant.

STEAMED EGG WHITE TOPPED WITH CRAB MEAT AND SHRIMP SAUCE

6 egg whites
1 cup chicken stock
1 tbsp cornstarch
1 tsp salt

Marinade
1 tbsp egg white
1 tsp cornstarch
⅛ tsp pepper

4oz shrimp
2 tbsp peanut oil

3-4 slices ginger
4oz crab meat

Sauce
½ cup chicken stock
1 tsp salt
2 tsp Chinese yellow wine
1½ tbsp cornstarch

Garnish
1 tbsp chopped fresh coriander
(cilantro)

Place the 6 egg whites, chicken stock, cornstarch and salt in a bowl. Beat the ingredients with a fork in one direction until they are thoroughly mixed and blended and transfer the mixture to a large, deep-sided dish. Steam the mixture over a medium heat for 5-6 minutes until it has set. Set aside.

Prepare the marinade and mix it with the shrimp.

Heat 2 tbsp peanut oil and add the ginger, discarding the ginger when it browns. Add the marinated shrimp and the crab crab meat to the pan. Stir rapidly.

Mix together the sauce ingredients and add to the pan. Keep on stirring. When the contents boil, pour them on top of the steamed egg white. Garnish with chopped coriander and serve.

PAN-FRIED EGG DUMPLING WITH MINCED PORK AND SHRIMP

6 eggs

Marinade
1 tbsp egg white (from main recipe)
1 tsp salt
1 tsp cornstarch
½ tsp sesame oil

4oz lean pork loin, minced
8oz shrimp, shelled and deveined
1 medium onion
1 cup peanut oil
1 tbsp chopped fresh coriander
(cilantro)

(Recipe continued on page 36)

葱花蒸蝦

STEAMED SHRIMP WITH
SCALLIONS AND LIGHT SOY
SAUCE
Cantonese chefs are
famous for their steamed
seafood. Here the essence
of the dish lies in the
combination of precise
cooking time and the
last-minute addition of
subtle seasoning elements
to maintain the freshness
of the ingredients.

STEAMED EGG-WHITE TOPPED
WITH CRAB MEAT AND SHRIMP
SAUCE
This is a comparatively
new dish created by
Cantonese chefs in Hong
Kong restaurants to meet
the tastes of a more
health-conscious clientele.
In both taste and
presentation it echoes the
current trend towards
lightness and elegance in
Hong Kong food.

STIR-FRIED SHRIMP AND
CHICKEN WITH ONION,
CUCUMBER AND FRESH
MUSHROOMS
This colorful stir-fried
dish brings together
ingredients of different
color, taste and texture.
The Chinese look for
interesting contrasts in
their food, whether in
flavour or texture, but
expect these contrasts to
be harmoniously
combined.

THREE DELICACIES STUFFED
WITH SHRIMP
In this dish the elements
of contrast are present to
a marked degree in
flavors that are both rich
and delicate. The bitter
melon, particularly,
provides a counterpoint
to the fullness of the chili
and shrimp.

Break the eggs into a mixing bowl, reserving 1 tbsp egg white for the marinade. Beat the remainder lightly. Make the marinade in a separate bowl and mix the minced pork loin with half of the mixture.

Clean the shrimp. Pat them dry and mix with the other half of the marinade. Keep refrigerated for 30 minutes.

Chop the onion and set it aside.

Heat the oil in a pan. Add the shrimp, stirring to separate, and remove them when their color has changed. Drain and set aside.

Sauté the minced pork for 2 minutes. Remove and set aside. Sauté the chopped onion for 1 minute. Remove and set aside.

Mix the pork, shrimp, onion and coriander with the beaten egg. Heat 1 tbsp oil in the pan and put 2 tbsp of the egg mixture in the pan to form one dumpling. Fry it gently over a medium heat, turning it over gently until both sides are nicely golden brown. Make two or three at a time and continue until all the ingredients are used. This simple but effective recipe will make eight or ten dumplings in all.

SHRIMP, HAM AND MELON ROLLS

8oz shrimp, freshly shelled (if not available, use frozen shrimp)

Seasonings
½ tsp salt
2 tsp cornstarch
½ tsp chopped garlic

1oz boneless, skinned, fresh bacon (3 tbsp)
2oz ham (¼ cup)
1½lb winter melon

Sauce
2 tbsp peanut oil
2 pieces of sliced ginger
1 tsp finely chopped garlic
8 tbsp stock
2 tsp soy sauce
2 tsp oyster sauce
few drops of sesame oil
3 tsp rice wine
½ tsp cornstarch (blended in water)

Chop and mince the shrimp. Mix the seasonings with the shrimp and beat the mixture until it is sticky.

Dice the fresh bacon into tiny cubes and chop and mince the ham. Mix both with the shrimp mixture.

Cut the winter melon into 1½ × 2 × 4in pieces and blanch the melon in boiling water. Remove and drain.

Spread a little of the shrimp mixture on each melon slice. Roll the melon around the mixture and place the rolls on a plate standing on a metal rack in a large saucepan. Steam the rolls vigorously for 10 minutes.

Make the sauce by heating 2 tbsp peanut oil in a pan. Add the ginger slices but remove them as soon as they become yellow. Then add the garlic and the other sauce ingredients. Stir when the sauce boils, stir again and pour over the melon rolls to serve.

桂林蝦丸

DEEP-FRIED SHRIMP BALLS SERVED WITH SWEET-AND-SOUR SAUCE

1¼lb shrimp, shelled and deveined	1 egg white
⅓ cup fresh bacon fat	2 tbsp cornstarch
2oz water chestnut	1¾ cups dried bread crumbs
	2 cups peanut oil

Clean the shrimp. Pat them dry and beat them with the flat side of a cleaver.

Dice the cooked bacon fat into tiny pieces and cut the water chestnuts into similar tiny pieces.

Put the beaten shrimp in a mixing bowl and add the egg white and cornstarch. Stir with a fork in one direction until the mixture is sticky and firm.

Add the bacon fat and keep on stirring until the mixture is consistent and sticky. Stir in the diced pieces of water chestnut and keep on stirring until the mixture becomes firm.

Lightly oil your fingers and palms and roll ¾ tbsp of the shrimp mixture into a small ball. Coat each ball with bread crumbs.

Heat the oil in a pan. Test that the temperature is correct by putting a thin slice of ginger into the pan; when it curls up immediately the temperature is right. Add the shrimp balls and fry over a high heat for 1 minute. Reduce the temperature to medium and fry for another 2 minutes. Turn off the heat and let the shrimp balls sit for 5 minutes in the oil. Remove and drain.

Reheat the oil and after 15 seconds return the shrimp balls and fry for 2 minutes. Serve with Sweet-and-sour Sauce (see below).

SWEET-AND-SOUR SAUCE BASE

5 cups rice vinegar	1½ cups tomato catsup
2 tsp salt	2 tsp dark soy sauce
2 cups brown sugar	

This recipe makes a useful sweet-and-sour sauce base that will keep for long periods.

Bring the vinegar to the boil. Add the salt and then add the sugar. Once the sugar has dissolved, add the tomato catsup. When the mixture returns to the boil, add the soy sauce.

This sauce base can be kept in the refrigerator in a covered container until needed. For use and to serve, add water and cornstarch and bring to the boil, stirring all the time until the sauce thickens and becomes translucent. It may be served with such dishes as sweet-and-sour-pork, spare ribs and deep-fried fish.

PAN-FRIED EGG DUMPLING

DEEP-FRIED SHRIMP BALLS
Deep-fried dishes such as this are familiar favorites in the west. A serving of sweet-and-sour sauce adds a complementary contrast of flavor.

PAN-FRIED EGG DUMPLING WITH MINCED PORK AND SHRIMP
This is really a type of Chinese omelet, but with an extra succulence and delicacy. Patience is the key to success in this dish — use low heat to avoid burning the dumplings.

SHRIMP, HAM AND MELON ROLLS
This dish has been aptly described as a new frontier in taste. Elegant and exotic to look at, it provides a deliciously surprising flavor that can be enjoyed at little risk to the waistline!

桂林蝦丸

SHARK'S FIN CONSOMME

1¹/₂lb shark's fin	1 cup good stock
2oz ham	1¹/₂ tbsp finely shredded ham
1¹/₂lb lean pork	1¹/₂ tbsp chopped fresh coriander
6 cups chicken stock	(cilantro)
3 slices ginger	

Soak the dried shark's fin in 4 pints boiling water overnight. The next day bring 1 gallon water to the boil and simmer the shark's fin for 6 hours. Remove it from the water and rinse under the tap for 30-60 minutes.

Blanch 2oz ham and the lean pork in 5 cups boiling water for 5 minutes, then place the meat, the chicken stock and ginger in a covered china container and steam for 3 hours.

Place the prepared shark's fin on a platter, add 1 cup good stock and steam for 20 minutes.

Divide the shark's fin into small individual portions, add the boiling stock and sprinkle with the finely shredded ham and chopped coriander. Serve.

SHARK'S FIN SOUP WITH CHICKEN WING STUFFED WITH HAM AND MUSHROOMS

1¹/₂lb dried shark's fin, skin and	4oz ham
bone removed	10 chicken wings
5 cups chicken stock	2 large black mushrooms
1¹/₂lb spare rib of pork	

Prepare the shark's fin, following the method given in the recipe for Shark's Fin Consommé. Set it aside.

Bring the chicken stock and an equal amount of water to the boil. Add the spare rib of pork and half the ham cut into thin slices. Simmer for 2 hours and set aside.

Steam the chicken wings for 20 minutes, remove the bones and set aside.

Soak the mushrooms in hot water for 30 minutes. Remove and discard the stems and then cut the caps into ¹/₄in strips. Set them aside.

Cut the remaining ham into slices ¹/₈in thick and cut each slice into pieces ¹/₈ × 1³/₄in. Set them aside.

Stuff the chicken wings with strips of mushroom and ham, place the shark's fin in a soup tureen and arrange the stuffed chicken wings on top.

Add the stock and steam for 1 hour. Serve.

蟹
黃
魚
翅

SHARK'S FIN SOUP WITH CRAB ROE SAUCE

1¹/₂lb dried shark's fin, skin and
   bone removed
1 cup peanut oil
6 slices ginger
the green of 1 scallion
roe from 2 female crabs
1 tsp sesame oil

1 tbsp Chinese yellow wine
4 cups chicken stock
1 tsp salt
2 tbsp cornstarch, softened in
   2 tbsp water

Prepare the shark's fin, following the method given in the recipe for Shark's Fin Consommé. Set it aside.

Heat two-thirds of the oil in a pan and add the ginger and scallion. Remove them when they have browned and turn off the heat.

Mix 3 tbsp oil with the crab roes, add the sesame oil and Chinese yellow wine, stir well and set aside.

Reheat the oil, add the shark's fin and chicken stock and simmer for 30 minutes. Add the salt and simmer for a further 5 minutes. Bring the contents of the pan to the boil again and stir in 2 tbsp cornstarch mixed with an equal amount of water. Reduce the heat, stir in the crab roes and serve.

SHARK'S FIN WITH CRAB MEAT IN BROWN SAUCE

1¹/₂lb dried shark's fin, skin and
   bone removed
8 tbsp peanut oil
4 slices ginger
1 scallion
4 cups chicken stock
8oz crab meat
1¹/₂ tbsp Chinese yellow wine

1 tbsp oyster sauce
1 tsp sugar
1 tbsp light soy sauce
¹/₂ tsp pepper
1 tsp sesame oil
2 tbsp cornstarch softened in
   2 tbsp water
1 tsp dark soy sauce

Prepare the shark's fin, following the method given in the recipe for Shark's Fin Consommé. Set it aside.

Heat the peanut oil in a pan. Add the ginger and scallion, but remove and discard them when they turn brown.

Add the shark's fin and the chicken stock to the pan and bring the mixture to the boil over medium heat. Add the crab meat and reduce the temperature to low.

When the mixture boils again add 1 tsp Chinese yellow wine and the oyster sauce, sugar, light soy sauce, pepper and sesame oil. Stir in the softened cornstarch, add the dark soy sauce and 1 tbsp Chinese yellow wine and serve.

清湯魚翅

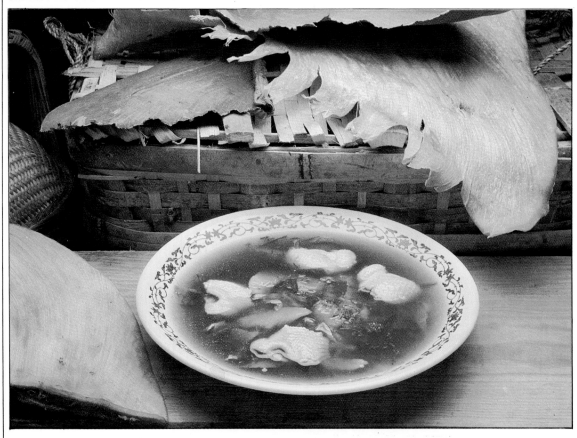

SHARK'S FIN SOUP WITH
CHICKEN WING STUFFED WITH
HAM AND MUSHROOMS
A traditional delicacy in
modern style, this soup is
a feast of flavor and
refinement. Shark's fin
may be bought in
semi-finished form in
Chinese food shops but
the process of
preparation is still a long
one. The effort, however,
is richly repaid by the
compliments of one's
guests.

SHARK'S FIN CONSOMME
This classic dish is
appreciated by
connoisseurs of Chinese
cuisine for its clarity,
flavor and the distinctive
glutinous texture of the
shark's fin.

SHARK'S FIN WITH CRAB MEAT
IN BROWN SAUCE
In this treatment of a
traditional delicacy, the
sweetness of the crab
meat, with its color,
provides a visual and
full-flavored contrast
with the shark's fin.

SHARK'S FIN SOUP WITH CRAB
ROE SAUCE
In Chinese culture, this
delicious shark's fin dish
symbolizes prosperity. It
is always the star of a
Chinese New Year
banquet menu, where it
appears as 'Prosperous
Shark's Fin'.

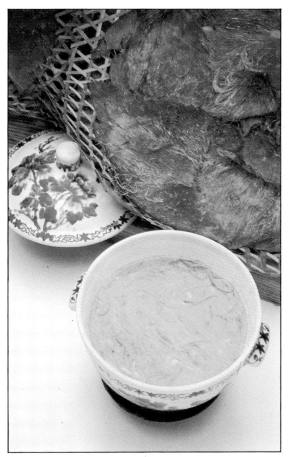

CRAB CASSEROLE

2 crabs (approximately 1¼lb each)	**Seasonings**
1 tbsp cornstarch	8 tbsp good stock
3 cups peanut oil	1 tbsp oyster sauce
2 tsp chopped garlic	1 tsp oil
3-4 slices fresh ginger	few drops sesame oil
2 stalks scallions	1 tsp sugar
	1 tsp rice wine

Clean the crabs and crush the pincers. Chop each crab into six pieces. Dry and dust with cornstarch.

Heat the peanut oil and fry the crabs for 1 minute. Remove the crab from the pan and drain the oil.

Heat the large pan or wok. Add the garlic, ginger and scallions and sauté for 15 seconds to release their aromatic flavors. Mix and turn them quickly with the crab before transferring the mixture to a clay container or casserole.

Add the seasonings. Cover the pot and cook for 2 minutes over a high heat, turning the contents from time to time.

Serve in the clay pot or casserole.

STIR-FRIED CRAB IN CURRY SAUCE

2lb crab	1 tbsp curry paste
2 tbsp cornstarch	1 cup chicken stock
2 cups peanut oil	2 tsp sugar
6 slices ginger	1 tsp salt
2 tsp chopped garlic	1 tsp Chinese yellow wine
10-12 scallions, cut into 2in pieces	

Place the crab on a chopping-board, belly-side up, and cut through the middle with a cleaver, but avoid cutting into the top shell. Chop off the claws, lightly crush the shell and set them aside. Lift off the top shell and clean the crab, discarding the 'dead men's fingers'. Chop the body into four or six pieces, depending on the size, and lightly coat the crab meat with cornstarch.

Heat the oil in a pan and fry the crab for 2 minutes over a very high heat. Remove, drain and set aside.

Heat 2 tbsp oil in the pan. Add the ginger, garlic, scallions and curry paste, stir and cook for 1½ minutes.

Return the crab to the pan, stirring, and add the chicken stock, sugar and salt. Cover the pan and cook over medium heat for 10 minutes, turning the contents once or twice to ensure that they are evenly cooked. Sprinkle with yellow wine and serve.

豉
椒
炒
蟹

CRAB WITH FERMENTED BEANS AND PEPPERS

2 crabs (approximately 1lb each)
2 red chili peppers
1 green bell pepper
4 slices fresh ginger
3 stalks scallions
2 garlic cloves
2 cups peanut oil (for frying crab)
3 tsp salted, fermented soya beans

Seasoning
1 tsp sugar
1 tsp salt
2 tsp oyster sauce
*¹/₂ tsp monosodium glutamate
  (optional)*
2 tsp rice wine

¹/₂ cup stock or chicken soup

Clean the crabs and chop the flesh of each into six pieces.

Mince the chili and the green pepper. Cut the scallions into ³/₄in pieces. Crush and chop garlic.

Heat the oil in a pan and add the crab, ginger and scallions. Fry for 2 minutes and remove from the pan to drain.

Reheat the pan to smoking point and add 1 tbsp oil. Fry the garlic and fermented beans for 10 seconds, then return the crab to the pan.

Mix the seasoning ingredients with the stock or chicken soup and add the mixture to the pan. Turn and stir the contents for 30 seconds and serve.

ASPARAGUS TOPPED WITH CRAB MEAT SAUCE

4oz crab meat
1¹/₄lb fresh asparagus
4 tbsp peanut oil
8 tbsp chicken stock
4 slices fresh ginger
1 garlic clove

Sauce
1 egg white
¹/₂ cup chicken stock
1 tsp sesame oil
2 tsp Chinese yellow wine
¹/₂ tsp sugar
¹/₄ tsp pepper
1¹/₂ tsp cornstarch

Steam a medium sized crab for 20 minutes. Scoop out the crab meat from the shells and set aside.

Clean the asparagus and cut the stalks into 1¹/₂in sections, discarding the tough part close to the roots.

Heat 1 tbsp oil and add the chicken stock to the pan. Cook the asparagus until the stock is almost dried up. Transfer to a plate and set aside to keep warm.

Heat 3 tbsp oil in the pan, add the ginger and garlic and when browned, remove and discard them.

Add the crab meat to the pan and sauté for 30 seconds. Mix the sauce ingredients, stir into the pan and bring to the boil. Pour the mixture over the asparagus and serve.

香汁炒蟹

STIR-FRIED CRAB IN CURRY SAUCE

There is an obvious south-east Asian influence in this Cantonese dish. Although, in general, Cantonese cuisine is subtle in character, there are hot and spicy dishes comparable to the Sichuan school.

CRAB CASSEROLE

A superb dish for the colder months of the year. The delicate flavor is typical of the Cantonese school.

豉椒炒蟹

CRAB WITH FERMENTED BEANS
AND PEPPERS
Fermented beans, more
commonly known as
black beans, are widely
used in Cantonese
cooking, usually with red
chili and garlic. Together
they make a unique spicy
sauce that is unmistakably
Cantonese.

ABALONE STEAK IN OYSTER SAUCE

2 cans abalone	*1 tbsp Chinese yellow wine*
3-4 tbsp peanut oil	*2 tbsp oyster sauce*
3-4 slices fresh ginger	*1 tsp sugar*
1-2 garlic cloves	*2 tbsp cornstarch*

Boil the abalone in the tins for 5 hours over a low heat in 6-7 pints of water before opening the cans. Cut the abalone in slices ½in thick. Save ½ cup of liquid in the cans to use as a base for the sauce.

Heat 3-4 tbsp oil in a pan and add the ginger and garlic, frying them until browned. Remove and discard.

Add the Chinese yellow wine and liquid from the abalone to the pan and stir in the oyster sauce, sugar and cornstarch mixed with 2 tbsp water.

Finally, add the abalone slices, stir well to mix with the sauce and serve.

Abalone is always one of the star dishes on a banquet menu. Canned abalone is recommended for this recipe as some of the dried varieties are expensive and complicated to prepare. If you wish you may take the abalone from the can without first boiling it, but you will have to cut it into thinner slices, not exceeding ⅛in, otherwise the texture will be too tough and rubbery for you to enjoy.

SLICED ABALONE IN OYSTER SAUCE WITH LETTUCE

1¼lb canned abalone	*2 tbsp oyster sauce*
⅔ cup peanut oil	*1 tsp dark soy sauce*
1 tbsp salt	*1 tsp sesame oil*
1¼lb lettuce	*1 tsp sugar*
2-3 slices fresh ginger	*4 tbsp chicken stock*
1-2 garlic cloves	*4 tbsp abalone stock*
1 tbsp Chinese yellow wine	*1 tsp Chinese yellow wine*
	1 tbsp cornstarch

Stand the unopened can of abalone in plenty of water and boil for 3 hours. Remove the abalone from the can, saving 4 tbsp juice to make the sauce. Trim the abalone into thin slices (⅛-½in) and set aside.

Heat 4 tbsp oil and the salt with 4 cups water in a pan. Bring to the boil and blanch the lettuce leaves for 1 minute. Remove, drain thoroughly and place on a serving dish.

Heat 6 tbsp oil in the pan and add the ginger and garlic.

Remove and discard the garlic when it has turned brown. Add the abalone slices and 1 tbsp Chinese yellow wine and sauté them lightly.

Add the remaining ingredients, stir and cook for 30 seconds over medium heat. Transfer to the serving dish with the lettuce.

You can make this dish more saucy by using all the abalone stock from the can and doubling the portions of the other sauce ingredients.

ABALONE, CHICKEN AND DUCK WRAPPED IN LETTUCE LEAVES

1¹/₂oz abalone
1¹/₂oz breast of chicken
1¹/₂oz roast duck
1¹/₂oz fresh chicken liver
1oz water chestnuts
2 large button mushrooms
3 stalks scallions
2 cups peanut oil
1¹/₂oz olive kernels
¹/₂oz rice-flour noodles
1 tsp chopped garlic
1 tsp chopped ginger

Seasonings
1 tsp oyster sauce

1 tsp monosodium glutamate (optional)
¹/₂ tsp salt
¹/₂ tsp sugar
¹/₄ tsp pepper
4 tbsp stock

3 tbsp chopped cooked ham
2 stalks fresh coriander (cilantro)
10 lettuce leaves
1 dish containing 3 tbsp hoisin sauce
1 dish containing 1 tbsp shredded ginger and 2 tbsp vinegar

Dice the abalone, chicken, duck, chicken liver, water chestnuts and mushrooms into ¹/₂in cubes. Cut the scallions into pieces ³/₄in long.

Heat a pan until it is very hot and pour the peanut oil into it. Fry the chicken, chicken liver and olive kernels for 15 seconds. Remove them from the pan, leaving behind the oil. Reheat the oil and add the rice noodles to the same pan. They should froth up into crispy noodles.

Remove them from the pan and drain on absorbent paper. Spread out the noodles on a serving dish.

Heat the pan again until it is very hot. Add 2 tbsp peanut oil. When hot, add the onions, garlic and ginger, and then the water chestnuts and mushrooms. Stir-fry for 1 minute. Add the abalone, chicken meat, duck meat, chicken liver, olive kernels and the seasonings. Stir-fry for another minute. Transfer from the pan to the plate, arranging them on top of the rice noodles. Garnish with the chopped ham and coriander.

The dish is eaten by wrapping spoonfuls of the dish in the lettuce leaves, which are spread with hoisin sauce and sprinkled with vinegar and ginger.

蟹
扒
露
笋

ASPARAGUS TOPPED WITH CRAB
MEAT SAUCE
Chinese chefs are famous
for preparing vegetables
in such a way as to
maintain freshness and
flavor. Here, the
combination of asparagus
and crab meat offers a
particularly successful
harmony of flavors.

SLICED ABALONE IN OYSTER
SAUCE WITH LETTUCE
Properly prepared,
abalone is a great delicacy
and is deservedly one of
the highlights of the
Chinese banquet menu.
The rich oyster sauce in
this dish enhances both
the flavor and texture of
the abalone.

蟹扒露笋

ABALONE, CHICKEN AND DUCK
WRAPPED IN LETTUCE
A good example of the
way in which Chinese
cooking makes optimum
use of ingredients. The
trimmings of abalone
steak inject new life into
this otherwise rather
ordinary dish. The
combination is set off by
the freshness and
crispiness of the lettuce.

ABALONE STEAK IN OYSTER
SAUCE
Abalone is unashamedly a
luxury item and a piece of
best-quality abalone steak
in a Hong Kong
restaurant would cost as
much as a meal for two in
London!

FRIED OYSTERS

12 large oysters
2 tbsp cornstarch (for cleaning
    oysters)
2 tbsp salt (for cleaning oysters)
1 tsp monosodium glutamate
    (optional)
1 tsp salt

Sauce
¹/₂ cup all-purpose flour
2 tbsp cornstarch

1 tbsp active dry yeast
1 tsp oil
³/₄ cup water

2 cups peanut oil (for frying
    oysters)

Dips
1 small plate of catsup
1 small plate of spiced salt

Rub the oysters thoroughly with cornstarch and salt and then wash them in water. Drop the oysters into a pan of boiling water until they are half cooked (this takes about 20 seconds). Dry the oysters carefully with a towel then mix them well with the monosodium glutamate (if used) and 1 tsp salt.

Mix the sauce ingredients, blending them together thoroughly.

Heat the peanut oil in a pan. Dip the oysters into the sauce and fry them until brown over low heat.

Serve with catsup, or prepare a dish of spiced salt by putting 1-2 tbsp salt and 1 tsp peppercorns in a pan over low heat until they start to brown; remove the peppercorns and keep the salt.

STIR-FRIED SCALLOPS WITH SNOW PEAS, CELERY, WATER CHESTNUTS AND BLACK FUNGUS

1lb scallops (fresh or frozen)

Marinade
1 tsp salt
¹/₂ tsp pepper
1 tsp sesame oil
1¹/₄ tbsp ginger juice
1 tbsp cornstarch

1oz dried black fungus (cloud ear)
8oz snow peas
8oz celery
4oz water chestnut

2 cups peanut oil
1 tsp salt
2 tbsp stock
2 tsp minced ginger
2 tsp minced garlic

Sauce
1 tbsp oyster sauce
1 tsp dark soy sauce
1 tbsp light soy sauce
2 tbsp stock
1 tsp sugar
¹/₂ tsp sesame oil
1 tbsp cornstarch
2 tsp Chinese yellow wine

Cut the scallops horizontally in half. Mix the marinade ingredients and add the scallops. Set aside.

家
鄉
妙
帶
子

Soak the black fungus in hot water for about 10 minutes.

Top and tail the snow peas, cutting them slantwise into 2 × ³/₄in pieces. Cut the celery into pieces the same size. Slice the water chestnut into ¹/₄in pieces.

Heat the oil in a pan until very hot: test by putting in a thin slice of ginger; if it curls up and browns immediately the temperature is right. Add the scallops, stirring to separate and prevent them from sticking. Turn off the heat and allow to stand for 30 seconds. Drain thoroughly and set aside.

Heat 2 tbsp oil in the pan. Add the snow peas, celery, water chestnut and black fungus, sauté and stir for 1 minute. Add 1 tsp salt and 2 tbsp stock and cook for another minute. Remove from the pan and set aside. Heat 1 tbsp oil in the pan. Add the ginger and garlic and, when the aroma rises, add the scallops and other ingredients. Stir rapidly over a high heat for 15 seconds.

Mix the sauce ingredients and add to the pan. Stir rapidly for another 15 seconds and serve.

STEAMED GROUPER WITH HAM AND MUSHROOMS

1¹/₂-1³/₄lb grouper or sea bass	5oz ham
2 tsp salt	4 slices fresh ginger
¹/₄ tsp pepper	4 stalks spring onion
6 tbsp peanut oil	2 tbsp light soy sauce
12 medium Chinese dried	2 tbsp Chinese rice wine or dry
mushrooms	sherry

Clean the fish, remove the bones and cut the flesh into about 12 evenly sized pieces. Mix the salt and pepper with 2 tsp oil and rub the mixture over the fish pieces.

Soak the dried mushrooms in hot water for 30 minutes. Remove and discard the stems and cut the caps slantwise into three thin slices. Cut the ham into thin slices of similar size.

Shred the ginger and scallions into matchstick-size pieces and arrange half of the pieces as a bed on an oval, heatproof plate. Place the fish pieces, alternating with slices of ham and mushroom, over the ginger and scallions and put the plate in a steamer. Steam vigorously for 10 minutes and pour away any excess liquid that has accumulated during the steaming.

Sprinkle the soy sauce and rice wine over the fish, ham and mushroom and lay the remaining scallion shreds on top.

Heat 5 tbsp oil in a small pan and add the remaining shredded ginger. Stir the ginger in the boiling oil for 30 seconds, remove and discard the ginger and pour the hot oil over the fish, ham and mushroom. Serve.

FRIED OYSTERS

FRIED OYSTERS

This is not unlike the western oyster fritter. Worcestershire sauce is an essential ingredient which gives the seafood the required fiery bite.

STIR-FRIED SCALLOPS WITH SNOW PEAS, CELERY, WATER CHESTNUTS AND BLACK FUNGUS

The combination of vegetables used here appeals to both eye and palate, providing a skilful contrast of colors, textures and tastes to offset seafood, meat or poultry.

酥炸生蠔

雲腿麒麟斑

STEAMED GROUPER WITH HAM AND MUSHROOMS
The fish is cooked here in the classical Cantonese manner. First it is cooked with a heavy dressing of freshly shredded root ginger and scallions. This layer is then removed and a fresh layer of the same vegetables is laid over it. At this point a quantity of superheated fat or oil is poured over the length of the fish to impact the flavor of the ginger and the scallions into the fish. Here the carved slices of fish are interleaved with slices of dried mushroom and ham, which further enhance the flavor of this popular and colorful party dish.

脆
皮
魚
卷

FISH SOUP WITH BEAN CURD, VEGETABLES AND FISH ROLLS

1½lb sole (use a fillet of 8oz for fish rolls (below), the rest for making the soup)
8oz spinach
2 cakes bean curd
1 tbsp peanut oil
4 slices fresh ginger

3½ cups chicken stock

Seasoning
⅛ tsp white pepper
½ tsp salt
1 tsp monosodium glutamate (optional)

Remove the fillet from the fish to make the rolls and chop the remainder into smaller pieces to make the soup.

Clean the spinach thoroughly and cut it into pieces 2in long. Divide each cake of bean curd into four pieces.

Heat the oil in the pan. Add the ginger and the fish bones and trimmings to sauté for 1 minute. Add the chicken stock and the same quantity of water to the pan, adding the bean curd when the stock boils.

Boil for 7 minutes, add the vegetables and boil for another 3 minutes. Add the seasoning and serve with fish rolls (see below).

FISH ROLLS

8oz filleted sole
4 medium dried black mushrooms
¼ tsp salt
1 tsp oil

Seasonings
½ tsp salt
1½ tsp cornstarch
½ egg white

1oz ham
1½oz bamboo shoots

2 cups peanut oil (to fry fish rolls)
½ tsp chopped garlic
½ tsp chopped ginger

Sauce
2 tbsp stock
1 tbsp oyster sauce
2 tsp soy sauce
1 tsp rice wine
1 tsp cornstarch

Cut the fish into pieces approximately 1¾ × 2½in.

Soak the mushrooms in a small bowl of hot water for 30 minutes. Add ¼ tsp salt and 1 tsp of oil to the mushrooms and steam them for 10 minutes. Shred the mushrooms, discarding the stems.

Mix the seasoning ingredients and coat the fish thoroughly with the mixture.

Slice the ham and the bamboo shoots to matchstick-size shreds about ¾in long.

Place a combination of the ham, bamboo shoots and mushrooms in the centre of each fish fillet. Roll the fish up around the mixture and dust with flour.

魚
卷
連
湯

Heat the peanut oil until very hot and fry a few fish rolls for 10-20 seconds until they become golden. Remove and set aside. Repeat until all the fish rolls are fried.

Reheat the pan until it is very hot and pour in 1 tbsp peanut oil. Add the garlic and ginger to sauté. Return the fish rolls to the pan. Mix the sauce ingredients and add to the pan, turning the fish rolls over in the boiling sauce over a high heat for 10 seconds. Serve as an accompaniment to soup.

STEAMED SEA BASS WITH BLACK MUSHROOMS AND CHINESE HAM

1¹/₂lb fillet of sea bass or any white fish

Marinade
1 egg white
1 tsp cornstarch
¹/₂ tsp sesame oil
¹/₈ tsp pepper
1 tsp salt

6 medium black mushrooms
2oz Chinese ham

6 stalks scallions
6 slices fresh ginger, shredded
¹/₂ cup peanut oil
1 garlic clove

Sauce
1 tbsp oyster sauce
1 tbsp light soy sauce
¹/₂ tsp sugar
1 tsp sesame oil
1 tsp Chinese yellow wine
1 cup chicken stock

Clean the fish and cut it into slices 2 × 1¹/₂ × ¹/₄in. Mix the marinade, add the fish pieces and set aside.

Soak the black mushrooms in hot water for 30 minutes. Remove and discard the stems and cut each mushroom into three or four slices. Set these aside.

Cut the ham into thin slices, about the same size as the fish pieces, and set aside.

Take four of the scallions, cutting them into 1¹/₂in pieces. Use only the white part and the part immediately next to it, discarding the roots and discolored stalks.

Place the remaining two scallions on a large plate. Arrange the fish, ham and mushrooms in layers — one piece of fish, one piece of ham, one piece of black mushroom — on top of the scallions until all the fish, ham and mushrooms are used. Sprinkle the chopped scallions and shredded ginger on top of them.

Bring 4 cups water to the boil in a wok. Put a wire rack in the wok and put the plate on top. Steam vigorously over a high heat for 5-7 minutes only.

Remove the plate of fish from the wok, drain, and set aside.

Heat the oil in a pan. Add the garlic but remove it when it has browned and discard it. Pour the oil over the fish, draining away any excess from the plate. Add all the sauce ingredients to a pan, stir and bring to the boil. Pour over the fish and serve.

脆皮魚卷

FISH SOUP

FISH SOUP WITH BEAN CURD, VEGETABLES AND FISH ROLLS
Chinese cooks abhor waste. This recipe, which uses one fish for two dishes, will meet with the approval of the budget-conscious.

SMOKED WHITE FISH FRENCH STYLE
Not strictly speaking French, this dish is a Hong Kong interpretation of a French classic recipe.

雲腿麒麟斑

STEAMED SEA BASS WITH BLACK
MUSHROOMS AND CHINESE
HAM
Chinese black
mushrooms, ginger and
soy sauce are sufficient to
give an authentic Chinese
flavour to an everyday
meal. If sea bass is not
available, other fish may
be substituted.

SMOKED WHITE FISH FRENCH STYLE

1¾lb white fish, such as turbot or
    flounder

Seasonings
4 soup spoons western sauce
¼ tsp white pepper
1 tsp onion powder
1 tsp sugar
1 tsp sherry

1 tbsp butter

Garnish
half a lettuce
2 tomatoes
4 pieces ham (about 4oz)
2-3 tbsp mayonnaise

Cut the fish into four big pieces. Mix the seasonings together and marinate the fish in the mixture for 7-8 hours or overnight.

Drain the fish and bake it in a moderate overn 350°F for 15 minutes. Butter the fish on both sides and bake for a further 10 minutes. Shred the lettuce and slice the tomatoes. Halve each piece of ham. Put the fish on a hot plate and garnish with lettuce, tomatoes, ham and mayonnaise.

To make western sauce, finely shred 4oz each of celery, carrot and onion and 2 bay leaves. Add the shredded vegetables to 1 cup chicken stock and cook over medium heat until the liquid has reduced by about 50 per cent.

STEAMED CHICKEN AND FROGS' LEGS WRAPPED IN LOTUS LEAVES

1lb chicken legs
8oz frogs' legs

Marinade
1 egg white
1 tsp salt
1 tbsp light soy sauce
1 tsp dark soy sauce
1 tsp sugar
2 tsp Chinese yellow wine

1 tbsp cornstarch
½ tsp sesame oil

4oz fresh straw mushrooms
2 scallions
1-2 lotus leaves (depending on
    their size)
1oz ham, sliced
6 slices fresh ginger

Chop the chicken legs into bite-size pieces and cut the frogs' legs in half, discarding the lower leg. Marinate the chicken and frogs' legs and set aside. Cut the straw mushrooms in half and cut the scallions into 1½in sections.

Blanch the dry lotus leaves in 2 pints boiling water until they are soft, remove, rinse under the tap and pat dry. Put all the ingredients in an even layer on the lotus leaves, wrapping them up firmly and neatly. Place the parcel on a heatproof plate and steam over medium heat for 35 minutes. Unwrap the parcel and trim the lotus leaves to fit the plate. Serve.

蝦
醬
全
雞

GOLDEN CHICKEN WITH SHRIMP PASTE

3-3½lb fresh chicken
2-3 tbsp shrimp paste (fresh
   shrimps finely minced)

Marinade
3 tbsp cornstarch

1 tbsp Mei Kwei Lu or dry sherry
2 tsp ginger juice
1 tsp sugar
few drops sesame oil

3 cups peanut oil

Chop the chicken into large, bite-size pieces and pat them dry.

Mix the shrimp paste with the marinade ingredients, and marinate the chicken with the mixture for 20 minutes.

Heat the peanut oil in a pan until it is very hot. Put in the chicken pieces and fry them for 2 minutes over a low heat. Remove the chicken and set the pieces aside while you reheat the oil to boiling point. Fry them again for 1½ minutes and serve.

ROAST GOOSE CASSEROLE WITH BAMBOO SHOOTS

10-12oz roast goose
7oz bamboo shoots
6 medium black mushrooms
⅓ whole piece of aged dried orange
   peel
1 tbsp peanut oil
6 slices fresh ginger
2-3 garlic cloves, crushed

Sauce
1 tbsp oyster sauce

1 tbsp light soy sauce
1 tsp dark soy sauce
½ tsp sesame oil
2 tsp Chinese yellow wine
1 cup chicken stock

1 tbsp cornstarch
1 scallion cut into 1½in lengths
1 tbsp chopped fresh coriander
   (cilantro)

Cut the roast goose into bite-size pieces and the bamboo shoots into wedge shapes.

Soak the black mushrooms and dried orange peel in hot water for 30 minutes. Remove and discard the mushroom stems and finely shred the orange peel. Set aside.

Blanch the bamboo shoots in 3 cups boiling water for 5 minutes. Remove, rinse under the tap, drain and set aside.

Heat the peanut oil in a clay pot and add the ginger and garlic. When the aroma arises, add the roast goose, bamboo shoots, black mushrooms and orange peel, stir and cook for 1 minute.

Add the sauce ingredients to the pan and enough water to cover the ingredients. Bring to the boil, reduce the heat and simmer for 45 minutes. Thicken the sauce with 1 tbsp cornstarch mixed with an equal amount of water. Add the scallion and coriander and serve.

蝦醬全雞

STEAMED CHICKEN AND
FROGS' LEGS WRAPPED IN
LOTUS LEAVES
A great summer dish
distingished by the
refreshing fragrance of
lotus leaves. The colors
— jade green, ivory and
ruby red — suggest a
Chinese painting.

GOLDEN CHICKEN WITH
SHRIMP PASTE
As in all fried chicken
dishes, the chicken
should be juicy inside
and crispy outside.
Careful heat control is the
key.

炒燒鵝鬆

ROAST GOOSE CASSEROLE
WITH BAMBOO SHOOTS
A good way to use the
stringier parts of the bird
which might be tough if
they weren't cut into
small pieces.

CHICKEN, ABALONE, BLACK MUSHROOMS AND BAMBOO SHOOTS IN A CLAY POT

8-9oz canned abalone

Sauce
2 tbsp oyster sauce
1 tbsp light soy sauce
1 tsp dark soy sauce
1 tsp sugar
4 tbsp chicken stock
1 tbsp cornstarch

2 stalks scallions, cut into 2in
  lengths
1¼lb chicken drumsticks

Marinade
1 tbsp light soy sauce
½ tsp sugar
1 tsp sesame oil
1 tbsp cornstarch

8-10 medium black mushrooms
8oz bamboo shoots
2 cups peanut oil
1 tsp chopped ginger
1 tsp chopped garlic
1 cup chicken stock
2 tsp Chinese yellow wine

Cut the abalone into slices approximately 2in thick. Mix the sauce ingredients in a bowl; add the sliced abalone and scallions.

Chop the drumsticks through the bone into bite-size pieces; marinade them.

Soak the black mushrooms in hot water for 30 minutes. Remove and discard the stems. Cut the bamboo shoots into wedges about 2in long.

Heat the oil in a pan. When it is hot, add the chicken and fry for 2 minutes. Remove and set aside.

Heat 2 tbsp oil in a clay pot and add the chopped ginger and garlic. When the aroma rises, add the chicken, black mushrooms and bamboo shoots, stirring all the time. Cook for 1 minute.

Add the chicken stock, bring to the boil, cover and simmer over medium heat for 10 minutes.

Add the sauce ingredients, scallions and abalone slices. Stir-fry for 30 seconds and sprinkle with 2 tsp Chinese yellow wine before serving.

QUICKLY BRAISED CHICKEN WITH CHILIES, GREEN PEPPERS AND BLACK BEANS

1 chicken (approximately 2lb)
3 green bell peppers
2 fresh red chilies
1 small piece dried orange peel
2 cups peanut oil
2 tbsp fermented, salted soya beans
1 tsp chopped garlic
3oz shallots, choppd
2 tsp rice wine

Seasonings
3 tbsp stock
1 tsp salt
1 tsp monosodium glutamate
  (optional)
1 tsp sugar
2 tsp dark soy sauce
1 tbsp cornstarch blended with
  3 tbsp water

Chop the chicken through the bones into large, bite-size pieces and dust with cornstarch.

Cut the peppers and chilies into slices, and soak the dried orange peel before shredding it.

Heat the pan until it is very hot. Pour in the peanut oil and fry the chicken until it starts to turn brown.

Heat a clay pot or casserole until it is very hot. Pour 2 tbsp peanut oil into it and add the chilies, peppers, fermented beans, chopped garlic and shallots to sauté, stirring them together until fragrant.

Add the chicken pieces and sprinkle with rice wine. Sauté for a further 30 seconds.

Blend the seasonings and add to the pot. Stir and cover the container to cook for 1½ minutes over a high heat. Keep the container covered until ready to serve.

CHICKEN, BAMBOO SHOOTS AND BLACK MUSHROOM CASSEROLE

1½lb chicken pieces or poussin

1 scallion, cut into 2in lengths

Seasoning
2 tsp salt
1 tsp sesame oil
½ tsp pepper
2 tsp Chinese yellow wine or dry
   sherry
1 tbsp cornstarch

Sauce
1 tbsp oyster sauce
1 tbsp soy sauce
1 tsp sugar
4 tbsp chicken broth

6-8 medium black mushrooms
2 cups peanut oil
4oz bamboo shoots, sliced
4 slices fresh ginger

1 tsp sesame oil
1 tsp Chinese yellow wine
1 tbsp cornstarch blended with
   2 tbsp water

Cut the chicken into bite-size pieces. Mix the seasonings together thoroughly and add the chicken pieces. Mix and set aside.

Soak the black mushrooms in warm water for 30 minutes until they are soft; remove the stems.

Heat the oil and deep fry the chicken for 1½ minutes over a moderate heat. Drain thoroughly.

Heat 2 tbsp oil in a casserole, add the mushrooms, bamboo shoots, ginger, scallion and the chicken and stir-fry over a high heat for 1¼ minutes.

Blend the sauce ingredients and add the mixture to the casserole. Bring to the boil and simmer for 15 minutes over a moderate to low heat.

Finally, add the sesame oil, yellow wine and blended cornstarch, stir well and serve in the casserole.

鮮
人
參
雞

CHICKEN AND BAMBOO SHOOTS

CHICKEN, BAMBOO SHOOTS
AND BLACK MUSHROOM
CASSEROLE
In spite of its exotic
name, this is a simple,
tasty casserole cooked the
Chinese way.

DOUBLE-BOILED FRESH
GINSENG FROM LIAONING
PROVINCE AND CHICKEN SOUP
The mysterious root
renowned for its
health-giving properties is
here used to make a
warming soup ideal for
winter nights.

66

粟米魚茸羹

QUICKLY BRAISED CHICKEN
WITH CHILIES, GREEN PEPPERS
AND BLACK BEANS
A rich and very tasty dish
distinguished by the
unique taste of black
beans.

CHICKEN, ABALONE, BLACK
MUSHROOMS AND BAMBOO
SHOOTS IN A CLAY POT
This casserole is lifted
into the luxury class by
the addition of abalone,
which has a strong and
distinctive flavor.

DOUBLE-BOILED FRESH GINSENG FROM LIAONING PROVINCE AND CHICKEN SOUP

2-2¼lb chicken
4 cups boiling water
⅓ cup chopped ham

1¼lb lean pork
1 fresh ginseng (approximately
  1oz)

Clean the chicken and blanch it in the boiling water for 3 minutes together with the ham and lean pork.

Drain the meat and put it with the ginseng in a heavy pot or casserole with a lid. Add just enough hot water to cover and steam for 4 hours over medium heat.

Serve by bringing the pot or casserole to the table. The chicken and pork should be sufficiently tender to allow diners to take pieces of meat with their chopsticks. Season to taste.

ROAST GOOSE

1 young goose (approximately 6lb)
1 tbsp soya bean paste
1 tsp five-spice powder
1 piece star anise
1 tbsp sugar
2 tbsp light soy sauce
2 tsp chopped garlic

1 tbsp Chinese yellow wine
6 cups boiling water
2 tbsp malt sugar
4 tbsp honey or corn syrup
4 tbsp vinegar
1 cup water

Cut off the feet and wing tips of the goose. (If a young goose is not available, use a duck.)

Blend together the soya bean paste, five-spice powder, star anise, sugar, soy sauce, chopped garlic and yellow wine and rub the mixture all over the inside of the goose. Tightly fasten the neck and tail openings with skewers or string to ensure that the mixture does not run out when the goose is hung.

Place the goose on a rack, breast up, and pour half the boiling water over it. Turn the goose over and pour the remaining boiling water over it. Pat the goose dry and set it aside.

Heat the malt sugar, honey, vinegar and 1 cup water together, stirring thoroughly to mix well, and brush the mixture all over the goose.

Tie a piece of string around the neck of the goose and hang it up in a draughty place for 1 hour to dry.

Pre-heat the oven to 450°F. Place the goose on a rack in a roasting pan (at least 2in deep) and roast the goose, with the breast side up, for 12 minutes until golden. Turn the goose

脆
皮
烧
鹅

over with a towel (avoid using a fork) and roast for another 12 minutes.

Reduce the heat to 350°F and, with the goose breast side up again, roast for 20 minutes. Reduce the heat to 300°F and roast for a further 10 minutes, then reduce the heat to 250°F and roast for a further 10 minutes.

Finally, increase the heat to 450°F again and roast for 10 minutes. You will have to watch closely at this point to avoid burning the goose.

You may either chop the goose into bite-size pieces and serve with a plum jam, or serve the crispy skin first, as with Peking Duck, and use the remaining meat to make two more dishes, Roast Goose Casserole with Bamboo Shoots (page 61) and Stir-fried Minced Goose with Lettuce (below).

STIR-FRIED MINCED GOOSE WITH LETTUCE

4 medium Chinese dried mushrooms	*¼ tsp pepper*
1lb roast goose meat	*1 tbsp light soy sauce*
4oz bamboo shoots	*½ tbsp yellow bean paste*
2 garlic cloves	*½ tbsp hoisin sauce*
2 slices fresh ginger	*½ tbsp sugar*
4 water chestnuts	*1 tbsp Shaohsing rice wine or dry sherry*
1 stalk scallion	*1½ tsp sesame oil*
4 tbsp peanut oil	*2 sprigs of parsley to garnish*
1 tsp salt	*12 lettuce leaves*

Soak the mushrooms in hot water for 30 minutes. Remove and discard the stems and coarsely mince the caps. Chop the goose meat, bamboo shoots, garlic, ginger, water chestnuts and scallion into a similar coarse mince.

Heat the oil in a pan or wok. When the oil is hot, add the ginger and mushrooms. Stir them in the hot oil for 30 seconds before adding the bamboo shoots, garlic and water chestnuts. Continue to stir and fry for 1 minutes, then add the scallion and goose meat, together with the salt and pepper. Continue to stir all the ingredients for 2 minutes, turning them over to ensure that they are all thoroughly cooked.

Sprinkle the soy sauce, yellow bean paste, hoisin sauce, sugar and rice wine over the pan, and continue to stir, turn and fry, over a medium heat, for 3 minutes. Add the sesame oil and serve, garnished with sprigs of parsley.

Diners help themselves to a couple of spoonfuls of the minced goose mixture. They place the mixture on a lettuce leaf, wrap it up carefully and eat it with their fingers.

STIR-FRIED MINCED GOOSE

脆
皮
燒
鵝

STIR-FRIED MINCED GOOSE
WITH LETTUCE
The use of lettuce leaves
to wrap up minced
poultry is very much a
Hong Kong innovation.
Traditionally, the
wrapping would have
been of pancake — but
this is now regarded as
altogether too heavy and
filling when presented as
a part of a Chinese dinner
which may consist of
more than a dozen dishes.
This dish is often
reproduced using chicken
or pigeon.

ROAST GOOSE
Although roast duck is
better known as a
Chinese dish, roast goose
is actually preferred by
Cantonese gourmets.

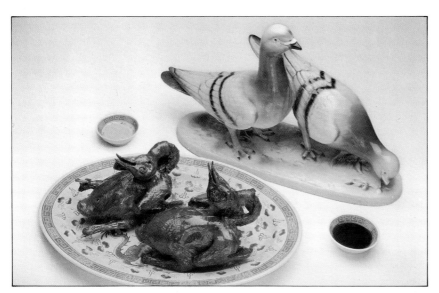

FRIED CRISPY PIGEON
The crispy skin is easy
enough to achieve, but
striking the right balance
of herbs and spices to
flavor the broth is a
delicate skill.

脆皮乳鴿

瑶
柱
火
鸭

ROAST DUCK WITH GARLIC

5-6 dried scallops	**Seasonings**
3oz of garlic	1 tbsp soy sauce
8-9oz roast duck breast	¼ tsp sugar
5oz spinach	1 tbsp oyster sauce
½ tsp salt	few drops sesame oil
2 tbsp oil	1 tsp cornstarch
	2 tsp rice wine

Soak the scallops for 3-4 hours and steam for 30 minutes. Fry the garlic until brown.

Cut the duck breast into 12 slices (each slice with skin attached) and arrange the meat in a big bowl (the skin to the bottom of the bowl), add a layer of scallops and finally the garlic. Steam for 45 minutes.

Fry the spinach with a little salt and oil and spread it out on a plate. Put the roast duck, scallops and garlic on top of the spinach and reserve the gravy.

Boil the gravy from the bottom of the bowl in a pan. Add the seasonings and stir into a sauce. Pour the sauce over the dish and serve.

FRIED CRISPY PIGEON

2 young pigeons	1 tbsp sugar
	5 cups water
Spicy stock	½ tsp white vinegar
½ Chinese dried orange peel	2 tsp malt sugar, molasses or honey
2 star anise	1 tsp cornstarch
1 tsp peppercorns	2 tsp water
3 slices fresh ginger	
1 scallion	2 cups peanut oil
2 tbsp dark soy sauce	
1 tsp salt	

Clean the pigeons.

Prepare the ingredients for the spicy stock. Bring the mixture to the boil. Reduce the temperature and put the pigeons into the stock to simmer for 7 minutes. Remove and drain the pigeons and pat them dry.

Mix the vinegar, malt sugar and cornflour with 2 tsp of water and rub the pigeons with the mixture. Hang the pigeons up to dry for 3-4 hours.

Heat the oil and fry the pigeons, turning them from side to side

脆
皮
乳
鴿

and basting them with the hot oil all the time to fry them evenly until the pigeons become brown, which takes about 5 minutes. Remove the pigeons and drain. Chop the pigeon in bite-size pieces to serve.

PIGEONS IN DARK SOY SAUCE

2 pigeons	1 cup dark soy sauce
5 cups water	¾ cup soy sauce
1 stick cinnamon	2 cups stock
2-3 slices liquorice root	2 tbsp Chinese yellow wine
3 slices fresh ginger	1oz rock sugar
4 shallots	

Clean the pigeons. Boil 5 cups water and blanch the pigeons for 2 minutes. Remove the pigeons from the boiling water, drain and pat dry.

Place all the remaining ingredients in a clay pot and bring to the boil. Allow to simmer over a low heat for 15 minutes before putting the pigeons into the pot to simmer in the sauce for a further 15 minutes. Let the pigeons color evenly by turning them over from time to time.

Cover the pot and turn off the heat, leaving the contents to sit for 30 minutes.

Dismember the pigeons and serve with the sauce from the cooking pot.

STIR-FRIED SUPREME OF PIGEON, BLACK MUSHROOMS AND BAMBOO SHOOTS

5oz supreme of pigeon (breast meat)

Marinade
1 tsp light soy sauce
½ tsp salt
½ tsp sesame oil
¼ tsp pepper
1 tsp Chinese yellow wine
1 tbsp cornstarch

5-6 medium black mushrooms
5oz bamboo shoots
2 cups peanut oil

1 tsp salt
1 tbsp stock
½ tsp minced garlic
½ tsp minced fresh ginger

Sauce
1 tbsp oyster sauce
1 tsp dark soy sauce
1 tbsp light soy sauce
2 tbsp stock
1 tsp sugar
½ tsp sesame oil
1 tbsp cornstarch
1 tsp Chinese yellow wine

(Recipe continued on page 76)

瑤柱火鴨

ROAST DUCK WITH GARLIC

ROAST DUCK WITH GARLIC
A good way to deal with left-over roast duck is to steam it until it is very tender, adding conpoy (dried scallops) and garlic for flavor.

STIR-FRIED SUPREME OF PIGEON, BLACK MUSHROOMS AND BAMBOO SHOOTS
Mushrooms and bamboo shoots form a combination that crops up time and again in Chinese cooking. Pigeon is used to make a change from chicken and is cooked in similar ways.

豉油王乳鴿

PIGEONS IN DARK SOY SAUCE
Only the best pigeons are used for this dish, which depends on the natural taste of the bird more than on seasonings.

PIGEON AND SHARK'S FIN IN A CLAY POT
An extravagant casserole compared to other clay pot dishes, but well worth the expense.

Cut the pigeon breasts into thin slices approximately 2 × 1 × ¼in. Mix together the marinade ingredients and marinate the pigeon slices. Set them on one side.

Soak the black mushrooms in hot water for about 30 minutes, remove and discard the stalks and cut the caps into thin slices. Cut the bamboo shoot into slices 1½ × ¾ × ¼in.

Heat a pan until very hot, add the oil and after 1 minute add the pigeon pieces. Stir to separate. Remove them from the oil and set aside.

Reheat the pan and add the bamboo shoot and mushroom slices. Sauté for 1 minute. Add 1 tsp of salt and 1 tbsp stock, cook for 2 minutes and set aside.

Heat 2 tbsp oil in the pan. Add the garlic and ginger and when the fragrance arises add all the cooked ingredients. Stir-fry for 1 minute over high heat before adding the sauce ingredients. Stir rapidly for 15 seconds. Serve.

CHINESE CABBAGE, MUNG BEAN NOODLES, DRIED SHRIMP AND SHREDDED PORK

1¼lb Chinese cabbage
4oz mung bean noodles
⅔ cup dried shrimp
2oz fillet of pork

Seasoning
1 tsp salt
2 tsp cornstarch
½ tsp sesame oil

½ tsp sugar

3-4 tbsp peanut oil
3-4 slices fresh ginger
4 cups chicken stock
1 tsp salt
2 tsp Chinese yellow wine

Cut the Chinese cabbage into ½ × 2in pieces. Soak the mung bean noodles and the dried shrimp in water for about 15 minutes until they are softened.

Shred the fillet of pork and mix the meat with the seasoning ingredients.

Heat 3-4 tbsp oil in a clay pot or a wok and add the ginger slices and shredded fillet of pork, stirring to separate. Then add the dried shrimps.

Add the Chinese cabbage, stir and mix well. Pour in the chicken stock and bring the contents to the boil. Reduce the heat and simmer for 15 minutes. Add the mung bean noodles and simmer for a further 2-3 minutes. Finally add salt and Chinese yellow wine and serve.

This simple recipe nevertheless has marvellous flavor. If you increase the quantities of chicken stock and wine, the dish becomes more soup-like in consistency. Either way, it should be served with a bowl of rice.

乳
鴿
吞
翅

PIGEON AND SHARK'S FIN IN A CLAY POT

4 oz soaked tiger shark's fin
1 king pigeon (approximately 1¼lb)
3 tbsp cooked shredded ham
2 cups peanut oil (to fry pigeon)
3 pieces sliced fresh ginger
2 stalks scallions
2 mushrooms
2oz roast pork

3 cups unsalted stock

Seasonings
1½ tsp salt
½ tsp monosodium glutamate
1 tsp sugar
1 tbsp oyster sauce

Soak the shark's fin in water overnight. Drain thoroughly.

Clean the pigeon and blanch it in boiling water for 1 minute. Drain thoroughly. Break up the shark's fin and insert the pieces and the shredded ham into the cavity of the pigeon. Close the cavity with a skewer.

Bring the peanut oil to high heat, add the pigeon and fry until the bird turns brown. Drain well.

Heat the clay pot, and pour 2 tbsp peanut oil into it. Add the ginger, scallions, mushrooms and roast pork to sauté until fragrant (about 2 minutes). Add the pigeon, unsalted stock and the seasonings, and stew gently for 2½ hours. Serve in the clay pot.

DOUBLE-BOILED PIGEON, HAM AND BLACK MUSHROOM SOUP

2 pigeons
8oz lean pork
6 medium black mushrooms
1½oz ham

3 slices fresh ginger
1 tbsp Chinese yellow wine
3 cups chicken stock
2-3 tbsp oil

Clean the pigeons thoroughly. Cut out the breast meat and save it for a Stir-fried Supreme of Pigeon.

Blanch the lean pork and pigeons in boiling water for 2 minutes and rinse under the tap for 1 minute.

Soak the black mushrooms in warm water for about 30 minutes until they have softened. Discard the stems and cut the caps into evenly sized pieces.

Put all ingredients in a heavy pot or casserole with a lid, add the stock and an equal amount of water, and cover and steam over medium heat for 3 hours.

(Double boiling is the favorite Cantonese way of preparing soup. The Cantonese believe that it not only makes the flavor richer but increases the mutritional value.)

SALT-BAKED PIGEON

鹽
焗
乳
鴿

SALT-BAKED PIGEON
This is a variant on the more usual Cantonese salt-baked chicken. The salt crust serves to seal in the flavor of the meat while making the outside deliciously crispy.

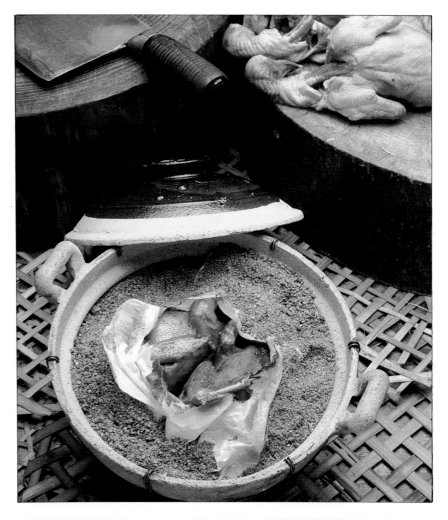

CHINESE CABBAGE, MUNG BEAN NOODLES, DRIED SHRIMP AND SHREDDED PORK
An inexpensive, homely dish with a semi-soup consistency. Dried shrimp — stronger in flavor than fresh — are used in China like stock cubes in the west, to provide a savory base. More than half the liquid is absorbed by the transparent mung bean noodles (known in the U.S. as cellophane noodles).

清湯伊麵

E-FU NOODLES IN SOUP
Adding shredded pork to
the soup makes it a
complete meal, but the
soup is delicious by itself
or as part of a meal.

DOUBLE-BOILED PIGEON, HAM
AND BLACK MUSHROOM SOUP
The basic savoriness of
this dish comes from the
pigeon; the ham and
mushrooms vary the
flavor. Double-boiling,
or slow steaming in a
closed pot, is an
alternative to boiling.

SALT-BAKED PIGEON

2 pigeons	1 tsp Chinese yellow wine
	1 tbsp dark soy sauce
Marinade	1 tsp ginger juice
1 crushed star anise	
2 shallot cloves	1/2 tsp sesame oil
1 tbsp shredded scallion	5-6lb coarse salt
1 tsp shredded fresh ginger	2 sheets wax paper
2 slices liquorice root	2 sheets foil

Clean the pigeons and dry them with a paper towel. Mix together the star anise, shallots, scallion, ginger and liquorice and rub the skin and the inside of the pigeons with the mixture.

Blend the yellow wine, soy sauce, ginger juice and sesame oil together, divide it and put it into the cavities of the pigeons.

Stir-fry the coarse salt over high heat for 2 minutes. Insert about one-third of the salt into the pigeon cavities, and cover the outside of the birds with the remaining salt.

Wrap each pigeon first with a piece of wax paper and then with the foil. Bake the wrapped pigeons in an oven at 350°F for 40 minutes.

Remove the paper and foil from the pigeons and shake them free of salt. To serve, cut the pigeons into bite-size pieces.

E-FU NOODLES IN SOUP

10 cups water	3 cups chicken stock
2 cakes E-Fu noodles	1 tbsp light soy sauce
2 tbsp peanut oil	1 tsp sesame oil
2-3 slices fresh ginger	3 tbsp finely shredded ham
8oz (3 cups) bean sprouts	2 oz Chinese white chives, cut into
1/2 tsp salt	1 3/4in lengths

Bring the water to the boil and blanch the E-Fu noodles for 2 minutes. Remove them from the water, drain, press with a towel and set aside.

Heat the oil in a pan and add the ginger slices. Remove and discard the ginger when it has browned and add the bean sprouts. Stirring, cook over a very high heat for 30 seconds, then add the salt, continuing to stir, and cook for 10 more seconds. Remove the ingredients from the oil and set them aside.

Heat the chicken stock in a pot, add the noodles and cook for 30 seconds. Add the soy sauce and sesame oil.

Transfer to a soup tureen and sprinkle the shredded ham on

top. Add the bean sprouts and white chives and serve.

This soup makes an appetizing snack or it can be served with other dishes as part of a meal. If you add shredded pork, it becomes a complete meal by itself.

BRAISED E-FU NOODLES WITH SHREDDED PORK AND MUSHROOMS

Sauce
1 tbsp oyster sauce
1 tbsp light soy sauce
1 tsp dark soy sauce
1 tsp sesame oil
¹⁄₂ tsp sugar

2oz fillet of pork

1 tsp cornstarch
2 medium black mushrooms
4oz chives
4 cups boiling water
12oz E-Fu noodles
3-4 tbsp peanut oil
tbsp shredded fresh ginger

Mix the sauce ingredients together in a bowl. Cut the fillet of pork into matchstick-size shreds and add 1 tbsp of the mixed sauce and 1 tsp of cornstarch. Mix well and set aside.

Soak the black mushrooms in hot water for 30 minutes. Remove and discard the stems and cut the caps into shreds. Set aside. Cut the chives into pieces 1¹⁄₂in long and set aside. Bring the water to the boil and add the E-Fu noodles. Parboil until soft. Remove, drain and dry the noodles with paper towels.

Heat 3-4 tbsp oil in a pan. Add the shredded ginger and fillet of pork and stir-fry for 1 minute. Add the mushrooms, stir and continue to cook for a further minute. Return the E-Fu noodles to the pan and add the remainder of the sauce. Stir and mix the ingredients together, simmering over medium heat until all water is absorbed by the noodles.

Sprinkle the chives over the noodles and cook for 30 seconds. Transfer to a plate and serve immediately.

SPARE RIBS WITH ORANGE

1lb pork spare ribs

Marinade
¹⁄₂ tsp salt
¹⁄₂ tsp sugar
¹⁄₄ tsp monosodium glutamate (optional)
2 tsp fresh ginger juice
1 tbsp cornstarch

few drops of sesame oil

2 cups peanut oil
1 tbsp Cointreau
4 tbsp orange juice
2 tsp cornstarch
¹⁄₂ monosodium glutamate (optional)
half an orange

(Recipe continued on page 84)

梅子鯉魚煲

SPARE RIBS WITH ORANGE
The fruity flavor goes
marvellously with the
spare rib: a really
delicious recipe.

蠔皇牛肉

BEEF WITH OYSTER SAUCE
This dish is a commonplace in Chinese restaurants everywhere — but, if you follow this recipe carefully, you will produce the dish at its very best.

BRAISED E-FU NOODLES WITH SHREDDED PORK AND MUSHROOMS
Once the pork has been stewed by the usual red cooking method, the gravy, with added mushrooms, is used to braise the E-Fu noodles.

Chop the spare ribs into portions 2in long. Prepare the marinade mix and use it to marinate the ribs for 1 hour.

Heat the peanut oil. Fry the spare ribs for 1 minute. Remove from heat but keep the ribs in the oil for 3 minutes, then remove them. Reheat the oil and return the ribs for another minute. Remove the ribs and drain away the oil.

Heat the pan and pour in 1 tbsp oil. Mix together the Cointreau, orange juice, 2 tsp cornstarch and the monosodium glutamate (if used), and add the mixture to the pan and bring to the boil.

Add the ribs to the pan and cook over a high heat for 10 seconds. Garnish with orange slices and serve.

The fruity flavor of the orange goes marvellously with the spare rib in this delicious recipe.

STIR-FRIED SHREDDED FILLET OF BEEF IN A BIRD'S NEST

Marinade
1/2 tsp sugar
1 tsp dry sherry or Shaohsing wine
2 tsp cornstarch
1/4 tsp sesame oil
1 tbsp soy sauce

6oz fillet of beef, shredded
2 potatoes, finely shredded
2 cups peanut oil

Sauce
1/2 tsp salt

1/2 tsp monosodium glutamate (optional)
1/2 tsp sugar
2 1/2 tsp oyster sauce
2 tbsp water

1 garlic clove, chopped
4oz pickled cabbage or bamboo shoot
1 red chili
1 green bell pepper
1 tbsp flour
1/2 tsp salt

Prepare the marinade, omitting the soy sauce, and steep the shredded fillet of beef for 20 minutes. Just before cooking, add the soy sauce and mix well.

To make the bird's nest, lay potato shreds in a large, perforated metal spoon or ladle, making a bowl shape by pressing the shredded potato down with another spoon. Deep fry in the perforated spoon until golden brown and crisp. Arrange on a dish.

Heat 2 cups oil in a pan. Add the beef and stir to separate. Turn the heat off as soon as beef changes color. Remove the beef and drain.

Mix the sauce ingredients and set aside.

Put 1 tbsp oil in a pan. When it is hot, stir-fry the garlic first, then add the pickled cabbage or bamboo shoots, red chili and green pepper (all shredded) and continue to fry for 1 minute.

Add the shredded beef and mixed sauce and stir-fry all the ingredients together for 30 seconds. Serve in the bird's nest.

蠔
皇
牛
肉

BEEF WITH OYSTER SAUCE

12oz beef steak
1oz fresh ginger
3oz white part of scallions

Marinade
1½ tsp ginger juice
1½ tsp rice wine
2 tsp soy sauce
½ tsp sugar
1 egg white
½ tsp meat tenderizer (optional)
1 tbsp oil

1 tbsp cornstarch

2 cups oil (for frying beef)
1 tsp chopped garlic
2 tsp rice wine

Sauce
1½ tbsp oyster sauce
1 tsp soy sauce
3 tbsp stock or water
1 tsp cornstarch

Cut the beef into very thin slices (1½ × ¾in).

Slice the ginger and cut the scallions into pieces 2in long. Mix the marinade ingredients and marinate the beef for 1 hour.

Heat a pan over high heat and add the oil, reducing to a low heat when the oil is hot. Add the beef and fry for 30 seconds. Remove with a perforated spoon and allow to drain.

Fry the ginger and scallions for a short while and remove.

Heat the pan again over high heat. Add 2 tbsp oil and fry the garlic, ginger and scallions for 15 seconds. Add the beef and sprinkle with rice wine.

Mix the sauce ingredients and add to the pan. Stir-fry for 30 seconds over a high heat. Serve, fresh and hot from the pan.

STEWED BRISKET OF BEEF WITH TURNIPS

2lb brisket of beef
2lb turnips
6 tbsp peanut oil
2 star anise
1 tsp peppercorns
2oz fresh ginger slices
2-3 garlic cloves
2 tbsp soy bean paste

Sauce
1 tbsp oyster sauce
2 tsp dark soy sauce
2 tbsp light soy sauce
2 tbsp cornstarch
1 tbsp Chinese yellow wine
1 tsp sugar

Blanch the brisket of beef in 5 cups boiling water for 5 minutes. Remove from the water, cut into 1½in cubes.

Peel the turnips, and cut them into 2in wedges. Cook them in 3 cups boiling water for 15 minutes, stirring all the time. Set them aside.

Heat a pan over high heat and add 2 tbsp oil. When the oil is hot, add the beef, star anise and peppercorns and cook for 3-5

鵲巢牛柳

STIR-FRIED SHREDDED FILLET
OF BEEF IN A BIRD'S NEST
The 'bird's nest' is made
of crispy shreds of potato,
which form a basket for
the meat. The soft texture
of the stir-fried beef
contrasts well with the
crackliness of the potato.

86

鵲巢牛柳

紅
炆
牛
腩

minutes, stirring all the time. Set aside.

Heat 4 tbsp oil in a clay pot, heavy saucepan or casserole. Add the ginger, garlic and soy bean paste and, when the aroma rises, add the beef and cook, stirring, for 1 minute over very high heat.

Add enough water to well cover the meat. Bring to the boil, lower the heat and simmer for 1 hour. Turn off the heat and allow to stand for 1 hour.

Bring to the boil again and simmer for 30 minutes. Add the turnips and sauce ingredients. Mix well and simmer for 15 minutes before serving.

STIR-FRIED SLICED BEEF, SQUID, FRESH MUSHROOM AND BABY CORN

5oz fillet of beef
5oz cleaned squid
7oz straw mushrooms, fresh or canned
7oz baby corn

Seasoning for beef
2 tsp light soy sauce
1/2 tsp sesame oil
1/2 tsp pepper
1/2 tsp sugar
1 tbsp cornstarch

Seasoning for squid
1 tsp fresh ginger juice
1 tsp Chinese yellow wine
1/2 tsp salt
1/2 sesame oil
1 tbsp cornstarch

1 cup peanut oil

1 tsp salt
1/2 tsp minced garlic
3-4 slices fresh ginger
2-3 slices scallions cut into 1 1/2in lengths
1 1/2 tbsp Chinese yellow wine

Sauce
2 tsp oyster sauce
1/2 tsp monosodium glutamate (optional)
2 tsp soy sauce
1/2 tsp salt
1 tsp sugar
1/4 tsp pepper
1 tbsp cornstarch
6 tbsp stock
few drops sesame oil
1 tsp Chinese yellow wine
4 tbsp peanut oil

Cut the fillet of beef into very thin slices 2 × 3in.

Divide the squid into pieces 3/4 × 2in, scoring the flesh on one side to form a diamond pattern. Cut the straw mushrooms and baby corns into halves.

Separately prepare the individual seasonings for the beef and the squid. Heat a pan, add 1 cup oil and heat for 1 minute over medium heat. Add the seasoned beef, stir to separate and remove with a perforated spoon after 75 seconds.

Add the seasoned squid to the oil, removing it with a strainer when it curls up.

Keep 1 tbsp oil in the pan. Add the baby corns, straw mushrooms, 1 tsp salt and stir well over a high heat for 30 seconds. Remove and set aside.

Heat the pan, this time over a very high heat and add 2 tbsp oil, the minced garlic and ginger slices. When the aroma arises, add the beef, squid and scallions, sprinkle 1 tbsp Chinese yellow wine over them and stir rapidly for 30 seconds. Add the baby corns and straw mushrooms. Stir for 30 seconds.

Blend together the sauce ingredients and add them to the pan. Stir for 10 seconds, sprinkle with ½ tbsp of wine and serve.

STIR-FRIED SHREDDED BEEF WITH PICKLED MUSTARD GREEN, GREEN PEPPER AND RED CHILIES

Marinade
½ egg white
1 tsp cornstarch
½ tsp sesame oil
1 tsp Chinese yellow wine
1 tbsp light soy sauce
½ tsp sugar

12oz fillet of beef
12oz pickled mustard green
12oz green bell pepper
2 red chilies
2 tsp sugar
3 tbsp peanut oil

1 tsp salt
1 cup peanut oil
1oz rice vermicelli
1 tsp chopped fresh ginger
1 tsp chopped garlic

Sauce
1 tbsp oyster sauce
1 tbsp light soy sauce
1 tsp dark soy sauce
1 tsp sesame oil
1 tsp sugar
1 tbsp cornstarch
¼ cup chicken stock

Prepare the marinade ingredients in a separate bowl. Cut the fillet of beef into matchstick-size shreds and marinate. Set aside.

Soak the pickled mustard green in water for 30 minutes. Chop into shreds and set aside. Shred the green pepper and red chili into 'double matchstick-size' pieces.

Heat a pan and add the chopped pickled mustard green, stirring to cook over a medium heat until quite dry. Add 2 tsp sugar and 1 tbsp oil, stir and cook for 30 seconds. Remove and set aside.

Heat 1 tbsp oil in the pan and add the green pepper and 1 tsp salt. Stir-fry for 2 minutes. Remove and set aside.

Heat 1 cup oil in a pan and add the beef, stirring to separate. Remove with a perforated spoon and set aside.

Heat the same oil for 15 seconds and add the rice vermicelli. It should expand and froth up immediately. Remove straight away and put on a plate to keep warm.

Heat 1 tbsp oil. Add the chopped ginger, garlic and red chilies and, when the aroma rises, return the beef, pickled mustard green and green pepper to the pan. Blend and add the sauce ingredients. Stir-fry over very high heat for 1 minute, place on top of the crispy rice vermicelli on the serving dish and serve.

酸
菜
牛
柳
絲

STIR-FRIED SHREDDED BEEF
WITH PICKLED MUSTARD
GREEN, GREEN PEPPER AND
RED CHILIES

This is called a Cantonese
dish but it can also be a
Sichuan dish, depending
on the amount of chili
used. The chili is fried
briefly in oil so that the
hotness pervades the oil.
The same can be done
with the pickle. The
shredded beef and green
pepper are cooked only
briefly. Adding vinegar
enhances the fieriness of
the chili, and as much as
a tablespoon of sugar
may be included in the
stir-fry. The whole dish
can be cooked in 4 or 5
minutes.

STIR-FRIED SLICED BEEF,
SQUID, FRESH MUSHROOM AND
BABY CORN

The success of this dish
depends on presenting
the four main ingredients
almost separately, so that
the different flavors,
colors and textures
remain distinct.

BRAISED MUTTON IN A CLAY POT

A slow-cooked dish probably introduced to Canton from the north (Peking or Outer Mongolia), where mutton is more common. The meat is cooked in a simple way and is served with one or more stronger-tasting sauces for dipping into.

STEWED BRISKET OF BEEF WITH TURNIPS

Beef and turnip make up a traditional Chinese combination. Brisket has a good flavor because of the fat it contains. It is cooked for almost three hours and produces a very tasty gravy, which is poured over rice.

羊腩煲

BRAISED MUTTON IN A CLAY POT

*3lb braising mutton (belly if
   possible)*
*8 pints water (for blanching
   mutton)*
3oz bean curd sticks
3oz bamboo shoots
3-4 tbsp peanut oil
3½oz sliced fresh ginger
3½oz leeks, cut into 1½in pieces
*1½oz salted fermented soya bean
   paste*
3 tbsp Chinese yellow wine
4 pints water (for braising mutton)
6-8 Chinese dried mushrooms
⅓ cup oyster sauce
2oz whole dried orange peel

3oz water chestnuts
4oz sugar-cane
3 lemon leaves

3 tbsp oyster sauce
1 tsp salt

Dip
*3 tbsp fermented bean curd or
   bean curd 'cheese'*
shredded lemon leaves
*gravy from mutton in clay pot —
   about 6 tbsp, enough to make
   one or two small dishes of dip*

Blanch the mutton in 8 pints water over a high heat for 10
minutes. Remove the mutton and chop it into large, bite-size
pieces.

Soak the bean curd sticks in water for 1 hour. Fry the bamboo
shoots for a short while until they turn bright yellow, which indicates that the water has been extracted from the shoots.

Heat the pan until it is very hot and pour 3-4 tbsp oil to the pan.
Add the ginger, leeks and soya bean paste into the hot oil to
release their aromatic flavors. Then add the mutton and pour in
the Chinese yellow wine. Stir and turn for 10 minutes.

Transfer the ingredients from the pan to a clay pot. Add all the
remaining ingredients and 4 pints of water. Simmer the mutton
for 1 hour over medium heat. Remove the sugar cane and lemon
leaves and add the oyster sauce and salt to taste.

Mix the ingredients for the dip. The mutton is served with the
dip, each piece of meat being dipped into the sauce before being
eaten. The sauce or soup is excellent with rice.

BRAISED BEAN CURD IN SHRIMP ROE SAUCE
WITH CHINESE FLOWERING CABBAGE

6 squares bean curd
*2lb Chinese green flowering
   cabbage*
2 cups plus 2 tbsp peanut oil
1 tsp chopped fresh ginger
1 tsp chopped garlic
1 tbsp shrimp roe

1 tbsp oyster sauce
1 tbsp light soy sauce
2 tsp Chinese yellow wine
1 tbsp cornstarch
4 tbsp chicken stock
1 tsp salt
1 tsp dark soy sauce
1 tsp sesame oil

红烧豆腐

Cut each square of bean curd into four pieces.

Remove the outer leaves of the Chinese flowering cabbage and blanch the heart for 3 minutes in 2 cups boiling, salted water with 2 tbsp oil added. Remove the cabbage and set it aside keeping it warm.

Heat 2 cups oil in a cap. Add the pieces of bean curd and cook until they are nicely golden in color. Remove them from the pan, drain and set them aside.

Heat 2 tbsp oil in the pan and add the ginger and garlic. When the aroma rises, add the shrimp roe, oyster sauce, light soy sauce, Chinese yellow wine, cornstarch and stock, stir and cook for 30 seconds. Return the bean curd pieces to the pan and mix them thoroughly in the sauce.

Sprinkle the salt, dark soy sauce and sesame oil over the pan, stir and serve with the cabbage.

POACHED KIDNEY AND LIVER WITH SCALLION AND GINGER

8oz pig's kidney	**Sauce**
8oz pig's liver	8 tbsp chicken stock
4 tbsp peanut oil	2 tsp dark soy sauce
2 cups boiling water	2 tbsp light soy sauce
1 tbsp salt	1 tsp sugar
2 tbsp shredded fresh ginger	1 tsp sesame oil
4 tbsp shredded scallion	2 tsp Chinese yellow wine

Slit open the kidney and remove the membrane and gristle. Cut the kidney into slices $\frac{1}{8}$in thick. Soak the slices in cold water and set aside.

Cut the liver into slices $\frac{1}{8}$in thick. Soak the slices in cold water and set aside.

Heat 2 tbsp oil in a pan, add the boiling water, bring to the boil and add the salt.

Add the kidney to the boiling water. Poach for 2 minutes, remove and drain.

Bring the water to the boil again and add the liver. Poach for 2 minutes, remove and drain.

Bring the water to the boil for the third time. Return the kidney and liver and add the shredded ginger and scallion. Turn off the heat and allow the ingredients to stand in the hot water for 4-5 minutes. Remove and drain.

In the meantime prepare the sauce. Heat 2 tbsp oil in a pan, add the sauce ingredients and bring to the boil.

Transfer the poached kidney, liver, ginger and scallion to a serving dish, pour the sauce on top and serve.

**POACHED KIDNEY AND LIVER
WITH SCALLION AND GINGER**
The use of scallion and
ginger in this dish makes
the taste of the variety
meats more acceptable.
The kidney is poached
only for a short time and
should still be slightly
crunchy.

**STIR-FRIED ASSORTED MEATS
WITH THIN RICE FLOUR
NOODLES IN CURRY SAUCE**
Sometimes called
Singapore noodles, this
dish shows the influence
of the south in the use of
rice, rather than wheat,
noodles and in the curry
flavoring. It is important
to release the flavor of
the curry by frying it with
the meat or with garlic or
ginger before adding
stock or sauce.

紅
燒
豆
腐

STIR-FRIED SHREDDED LAMB,
BAMBOO SHOOTS, BLACK
MUSHROOMS AND GREEN
PEPPER ON CRISPY FRIED RICE
NOODLES
Here the flavor of the
north, in the form of
lamb, is combined with
the texture of the south,
in the form of rice
noodles fried until they
are almost as crispy as a
bird's nest.

BRAISED BEAN CURD IN SHRIMP
ROE SAUCE WITH CHINESE
FLOWERING CABBAGE
Bean curd tastes very
bland unless cooked with
strongly flavored foods.
Here shrimp roes provide
the savory taste.

STIR-FRIED SHREDDED LAMB, BAMBOO SHOOTS, BLACK MUSHROOMS AND GREEN PEPPER ON CRISPY FRIED RICE NOODLES

1¼lb fillet of lamb

Marinade
1 egg white
2 tsp cornstarch
1 tbsp light soy sauce
1 tsp sugar
1 tsp Chinese yellow wine
1 tsp sesame oil

4 medium black mushrooms
12oz bamboo shoots
1 green bell pepper
2 cups peanut oil
1oz dried rice vermicelli noodles

1½ tsp chopped garlic
1½ tsp chopped fresh ginger

Sauce
1 tbsp oyster sauce
1 tbsp light soy sauce
½ tsp sugar
½ tsp sesame oil
1 tbsp Chinese yellow wine
½ cup chicken stock
1 tbsp cornstarch

1 tbsp finely shredded lime leaves
1 tbsp chopped coriander

Shred the lamb into matchstick-size pieces and mix well with the marinade. Set aside.

Soak the black mushrooms in hot water for 30 minutes. Cut away and discard the stems and squeeze the mushrooms to remove any excess water. Shred the caps and set aside.

Finely chop the bamboo shoots and green pepper. Blanch the bamboo shoots in 4 cups boiling water for 2 minutes. Remove and rinse under tap. Drain and set aside.

Heat the oil in a pan. Add the lamb and, after 75 seconds, stir to separate. Remove and set aside.

Add the dried rice noodles to the hot oil, removing them as soon as they fluff up (it takes only an instant). Place them as a bed on a large platter and keep warm.

Heat 3-4 tbsp oil in the pan and add the garlic and ginger. When the aroma arises, add the black mushrooms, green pepper and bamboo shoots and sauté for 1 minute. Return the lamb and stir rapidly over a very high heat for 30 seconds.

Add the sauce ingredients and continue to stir over a very high heat for another 30 seconds. Transfer to the platter and place on top of the noodles. Add the lime leaves and coriander and serve.

STIR-FRIED ASSORTED MEATS WITH THIN RICE-FLOUR NOODLES IN CURRY SAUCE

Marinade
1 tbsp egg white (from main recipe)

1 tsp salt
2 tsp cornstarch
½ tsp sesame oil

星
洲
炒
米
粉

15oz dried rice-flour noodles (rice vermicelli)
2 eggs
4oz fillet of pork
4oz shrimp, shelled and deveined
1 green bell pepper
1 red chili
7 tbsp peanut oil
1 tbsp chopped scallion

Curry sauce
1 tbsp curry paste
1 tsp chopped garlic
1 tsp sugar
2 tbsp light soy sauce
$\frac{1}{4}$ cup chicken stock
1 tbsp chopped coriander (cilantro)

Soak the dried rice-flour noodles in 6 cups cold water for 15 minutes. Drain and set aside.

Break 2 eggs into a mixing bowl, taking 1 tbsp of egg white for the marinade. Beat the remainder lightly and set aside. Make the marinade in a separate bowl.

Cut the fillet of pork into matchstick-size shreds and mix with half of the marinade. Set aside.

Clean the shrimps, pat them dry and mix with the other half of the marinade. Keep refrigerated for 30 minutes.

Cut the green pepper and red chili into thin shreds. Set aside.

Heat 2 tbsp oil. Stir-fry the chopped scallion until nicely browned; remove and set aside. Add the shrimp and pork, stir-frying them for 1 minute. Remove and set aside.

Make the curry sauce by heating 1$\frac{1}{2}$ tbsp oil in a pan. Add the garlic and curry paste. When the aroma rises, add the sugar, soy sauce and chicken stock. Bring to the boil, transfer to a bowl and set aside.

Heat 3 tbsp oil in a pan until very hot. Add the rice noodles and stir, turning the noodles over with the help of chopsticks. Stir-fry over a high heat for 3 minutes. Transfer to a plate and set aside.

Add 1 tbsp oil to the pan. Fry the beaten egg until partially set and add the green pepper and red chili. Keep stirring.

Return the shrimp and pork, and stir. Add the rice noodles to the pan and the curry sauce, stirring vigorously over a high heat for 3 minutes. Transfer to a plate, place the fried scallion and chopped coriander on top and serve.

WONTON SOUP

40 wontons (see Deep-fried Wonton with Sweet-and-sour Sauce page 100; increase the quantities accordingly)
1$\frac{1}{4}$ tbsp dried shrimp
1 tbsp peanut oil
4 slices fresh ginger

4 cups chicken stock
2 tsp sugar
2 tsp sesame oil
4-6 tsp light soy sauce
2 tbsp chopped scallions

(Recipe continued on page 100)

呑
麵
油
菜

WONTON SOUP AND POACHED
VEGETABLES WITH OYSTER
SAUCE
Wonton soup (see also
right) is very popular in
Canton, where it is often
served in tea houses to
accompany *dimsum*
(savory snacks).
Poaching need not be
done in water — hot oil
may be used instead. In
the north seafood would
be used for flavor. The
Cantonese, however, use
oyster sauce and perhaps
a touch of seasame oil.

DEEP-FRIED WONTON
This is a favorite.Chinese
starter for a party dinner.
Deep frying makes the
wonton very crispy.
Sweet-and-sour sauce is
used for dipping or
poured over the wonton.

錦鹵炸雲吞

呑
麵
油
菜

Make and wrap the wontons.

Soak the dried shrimp in 1 cup hot water for 30 minutes.

Heat 1 tbsp oil in a pot or casserole and add the ginger and dried shrimp, stirring until the aroma rises. Add the chicken stock plus the water used to soak the shrimp. Bring the contents to the boil, reduce the heat and simmer for 30 minutes. Add the sugar and keep warm in the pot.

Use four or six soup bowls and put into each $\frac{1}{4}$ tsp sesame oil, 1 tsp light soy sauce and 1 tsp chopped scallion. Set the bowls aside.

Bring 20 cups water to the boil. Add the wonton. Reduce the heat to medium and simmer for 5 minutes. Remove with a perforated spoon and divide them equally among the soup bowls. Add the soup and serve.

POACHED VEGETABLES WITH OYSTER SAUCE

2lb Chinese greens (flowering cabbage, Chinese spinach or lettuce)	3-4 tbsp peanut oil
	3-4 tbsp oyster sauce

Clean the vegetables. If you are using Chinese greens or Chinese kale, remove and discard the flowers and tough woody stem.

Bring the water used to poach the wontons to the boil. Put in the vegetables and cook for 3-5 minutes (if you are using lettuce cook for only 1 minute). Remove and cut into 2in pieces.

Place the vegetables on a plate, add boiling peanut oil and oyster sauce and serve.

Instead of oyster sauce I always use 1 tbsp of light and 1 tbsp of dark soy sauce and like the taste even more.

DEEP-FRIED WONTON ACCOMPANIED BY ASSORTED MEAT IN SWEET-AND-SOUR SAUCE

Filling

4oz fillet of pork	2oz roast duck meat
2 tbsp pork fat	2oz prepared cooked squid
20-30 shrimp, shelled and deveined	1 medium onion
	2-3 medium tomatoes
1 tsp salt	2 hard-boiled eggs
$\frac{1}{8}$ tsp pepper	3 cups peanut oil
1 tsp sesame oil	1 tsp chopped ginger
	1 tsp chopped garlic
	2 tbsp cooked shrimp
20-30 wonton wrappers	$1\frac{1}{2}$ cups sweet-and-sour sauce (see
$\frac{1}{2}$ egg white	page 37)
$\frac{1}{4}$ cup diced cooked chicken	

錦
鹵
炸
雲
吞

This is an excellent recipe for injecting new life into leftovers.

Dice the fillet of pork and the pork fat into small pieces and mix thoroughly with the other ingredients for the filling.

Place 1 tsp filling in the center of one wonton wrapper. Wet the opposite corners of the wrapper with egg white and gather the four corners of the wrapper together, squeezing them gently to form a small ball. Repeat the process until all the filling and wrappers are used. Set aside.

Cut the cooked chicken, roast duck and the squid into bite-sized pieces. Set aside. Cut the onion into wedges, pull the slices apart and set aside. Cut the tomatoes into wedges and each hard-boiled egg into four pieces.

Heat the oil until hot. Add the wonton and deep-fry for 1 minute. Turn off the heat and let them cook in oil for 3 minutes before removing them. Increase the heat to bring the oil back to a high temperature again and fry the wonton for another minute. Remove, drain and transfer them to a serving dish.

Heat 2 tbsp oil in a pan. Add the ginger, garlic and onion and sauté for 1 minute. Add the chicken, roast duck, shrimp and squid and, stirring, cook for 30 seconds. Add the sweet-and-sour sauce.

The diners dip the crispy wonton into the sweet-and-sour sauce before eating them.

FRESH MUSHROOMS AND BAMBOO SHOOTS IN SHRIMP ROE SAUCE

14oz fresh or canned straw mushrooms
14oz bamboo shoots
1 cup peanut oil
1 garlic clove
4 slices fresh ginger
1 tbsp dried shrimp roe (if not available use bottled shrimp sauce)
1 tsp salt
1 tsp sugar

Sauce
1 tbsp oyster sauce
1 tbsp light soy sauce
1 tsp dark soy sauce
½ tsp sugar
1 tsp sesame oil
1 tsp Chinese yellow wine
1½ tbsp cornstarch
½ cup chicken stock

Cut the mushrooms in half, and cut the bamboo shoots into slices $1 \times 2 \times \frac{1}{8}$in.

Blanch the bamboo shoots in 2 cups boiling water for 5 minutes. Remove and set aside. (If you are using canned bamboo shoots this is not necessary.)

Blanch the mushrooms in boiling water for 1 minute. (Again, this is not necessary if you are using canned mushrooms.) Remove and set aside.

COLORFUL BEAN SPROUTS

七彩銀芽

COLORFUL BEAN SPROUTS

The bright colors of the vegetables used in this dish give it great visual appeal. Bean sprouts are a handy vegetable because they grow easily indoors all year round and are pleasantly crunchy, but they can be insipid on their own. Ginger, scallion, sesame and soy sauce can all be used to add flavor.

FRESH MUSHROOMS AND BAMBOO SHOOTS IN SHRIMP ROE SAUCE

Mushrooms have a fairly distinctive flavor in themselves, particularly if the dried kind are used, but the taste of this dish is made even stronger by the addition of shrimp roe.

温公齋煲

VEGETARIAN CASSEROLE
Any number of vegetables
can be combined in this
casserole, including root
vegetables, leafy
vegetables, bean sprouts,
bamboo shoots or
eggplant. They are
cooked in meat stock or
orange stock, and mung
bean noodles or
transparent noodles, and
perhaps bean curd, may
be added. The resulting
semi-soup is a light
accompaniment to
heavier dishes.

蝦
子
嫩
笋
鮮
菇

Heat the oil in a pan. Add the bamboo shoots and fry for 1 minute, then add the mushrooms and fry for 1 minute. Remove, drain and set aside.

Heat 3-4 tbsp oil in a pan and add the ginger and garlic. When they have browned, remove them with a perforated spoon and discard.

Add the dried shrimp roes (or 2½ tsp shrimp sauce) and return the bamboo shoots and mushrooms to the pan. Add 1 tsp salt and 1 tsp sugar, stirring quickly, and cook for 1 minute.

Add the sauce ingredients, stirring continually over a high heat until the liquid is reduced to half. Serve hot.

VEGETARIAN CASSEROLE

8oz eggplant	2 tbsp red fermented bean curd
4oz French beans	2 cups chicken stock or water
8oz Chinese cabbage	2 pieces fried bean curd
6 medium black mushrooms	1 tsp salt
2oz mung bean noodles	1½ tbsp cornstarch blended with
1 cup peanut oil	1½ tbsp water
4 pieces sweet dried bean curd	1 tsp Chinese yellow wine
4 slices fresh ginger	1 tsp sesame oil
1 tsp chopped garlic	

Cut the eggplant into long, thick strips, the French beans in half and the cabbage lengthways into quarters.

Soak the black mushrooms in hot water for 30 minutes. Remove and discard the stems and cut the caps in half.

Soak the mung bean noodles in hot water for 10 minutes.

Heat the oil in a pan and fry all the vegetables for 1 minute over a high heat. Remove, drain and set aside.

Sauté the sweet dried bean curd over a low heat until slightly browned. Remove and set aside.

Heat 2 tbsp oil in a clay pot and add the ginger and garlic. Break the fermented red bean curd into pieces and add 2 tbsp to the pot, stirring over a high heat to release the aroma.

Place all the vegetables in the clay pot and cook, stirring continuously, for 2 minutes. Add the chicken stock or water, place the fried bean curd and sweet dried bean curd sheets on top of the vegetables and bring to the boil. Cover the pot, lower the heat and simmer for 10 minutes.

Add the mung bean noodles and salt, re-cover the pot and cook for another 2 minutes over high heat. Stir in the softened cornstarch, add the Chinese yellow wine and sesame oil and serve.

Any kind of vegetables may be used in this recipe, but if you choose a delicate vegetable, such as lettuce, add it at the last minute. This is an excellent accompaniment for rice.

七
彩
銀
芽

COLORFUL BEAN SPROUTS

3 pieces dried, spiced bean curd	**Seasonings**
2 bell peppers	*2 tsp oyster sauce*
2 fresh red chili peppers	*1 tsp monosodium glutamate*
1¹/₂ oz salted sour cabbage	*(optional)*
2oz leeks	*2 tsp soy sauce*
1 tsp sugar	*¹/₂ tsp salt*
4 tbsp peanut oil	*1 tsp sugar*
1¹/₂ tsp chopped garlic	*¹/₄ tsp pepper*
1¹/₂ tsp chopped ginger	*1 tbsp cornstarch*
1³/₄ cups bean sprouts	*4 tbsp stock*
	few drops of sesame oil
	2 tsp rice wine

Cut the bean curd, bell peppers, chilies and salted sour cabbage into matchstick-size shreds, and cut the leeks slantwise into 2in slices. Mix the cabbage with 1 tsp sugar.

Heat the pan until it is very hot and pour 1 tsp peanut oil into it. Add ¹/₂ tsp garlic and ¹/₂ tsp ginger. Stir-fry the bean sprouts for 30 seconds and put them on one side.

Reheat the pan until it is very hot and pour in 3 tbsp peanut oil. Add 1 tsp garlic and 1 tsp ginger and sauté until fragrant. Add the shredded bean curd, chilies and bell peppers and stir-fry over a high heat for 30 seconds. Add the bean sprouts and leeks. Stir-fry for another 30 seconds. Add the seasonings and continue to stir-fry for 10 seconds. Sprinkle with rice wine and serve.

FRIED MILK DAI LIANG COUNTY STYLE

2 cups oil (for frying noodles and	*1 tbsp cornstarch*
olive kernels)	*¹/₂ tsp salt*
2oz olive kernels	*3 tbsp oil*
1oz rice-flour noodles	*2¹/₂oz crab meat*
1¹/₄ cups fresh milk	
³/₄ cup unsweetened evaporated	**Garnish**
milk	*2 tsp chopped ham*
7 egg whites	*2 tsp chopped coriander (cilantro)*

Pour 2 cups oil into a pan. When the oil is hot, fry the olive kernels for 5 seconds over medium heat. Remove the kernels and immediately add the dry rice noodles. As soon as they froth up and float, remove the noodles, drain away the oil on absorbent paper and put them on a serving dish to keep warm.

In a bowl mix together the fresh milk, evaporated milk, egg whites, cornstarch and salt. Heat the pan until it is very hot and add

珊
瑚
荳
腐

CRISPY-COATED CORAL BEAN
CURD
The bean curd is deep
fried briefly so that it is
firm enough to pick up
with chopsticks and is
dipped into the sauce.

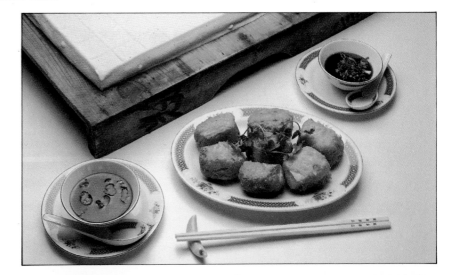

SWEET BIRD'S NEST AND
GINSENG SOUP
The contrast in this dish
lies in the cost of the
ingredients. Ginseng of
the best quality can be
very expensive, and the
finest bird's nest actually
costs more than its
weight in gold. The sweet
soup, however, costs next
to nothing, being
basically rock sugar syrup
thickened with cornstarch

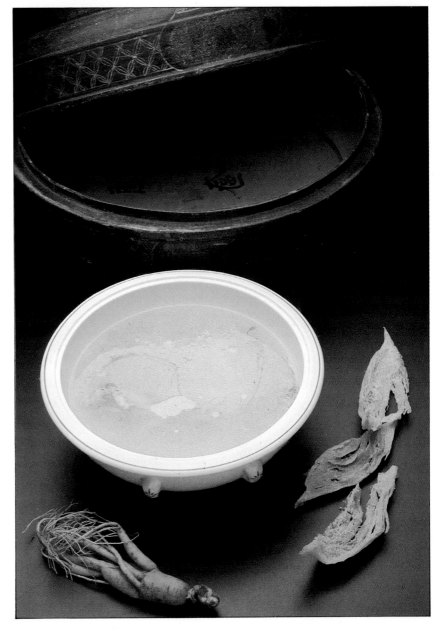

鴛
鴦
飯

YIN AND YANG RICE
Two colors of rice — the
one plain white, the other
colored with tomato
paste — are used in this
dish to form the Taoist
symbol, in which the
opposites yin and yang
form a complementary
whole.

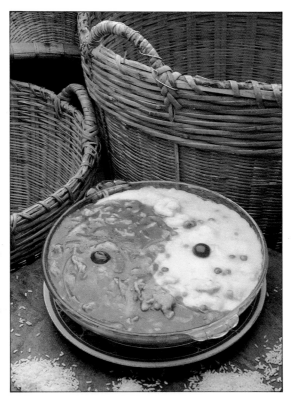

FRIED MILK DAI LIANG COUNTY
STYLE
It is actually the skin of
the milk that is fried. Milk
thickened with cornstarch
is cooked until the skin is
thick. The skin can then
be skimmed off and fried
on its own or used as a
rich batter to coat meat
or poultry.

大
良
炒
鮮
奶

3 tbsp oil. Then add the crab meat, olive kernels and milk mixture. Scrape the materials from the bottom and sides of the pan towards the center until the ingredients are set. Remove from the pan and spread over the noodles. Garnish and serve.

SWEET BIRD'S NEST AND GINSENG SOUP

1½oz bird's nest	*4 cups boiling water*
1 fresh ginseng root	*4 tbsp sugar*

Soak the bird's nest in hot water for 4-5 hours.

Clean the ginseng root, cut it into thin slices and place the slices and boiling water in a china or porcelain container with a lid. Steam for 1 hour. You may prefer to use the ginseng root whole; if so, steam it for 2 hours.

Add the sugar, stirring to dissolve, and then the bird's nest. Steam for 5 minutes and serve.

YIN AND YANG RICE

Marinade	*1 tsp salt*
1 egg white	*1 tsp chopped ginger*
1 tbsp cornstarch	*1 tsp chopped garlic*
1 tsp sesame oil	
1 tsp salt	**White sauce**
	8 tbsp chicken stock
8oz chicken breast	*2 tbsp milk*
9oz shrimp, shelled and deveined	*1 tbsp cornstarch*
4 tbsp peanut oil	*1 tsp salt*
1 tbsp shredded fresh ginger	
2 eggs, beaten	**Red sauce**
8oz cold plain cooked rice	*1½ tbsp tomato catsup*
2 tbsp light soy sauce	*8 tbsp chicken stock*
1 cup chicken stock	*1 tbsp cornstarch*
1 cup peanut oil	*1 tsp sugar*
½ cup peas	*1 tbsp light soy sauce*

Mix together the marinade ingredients in a bowl. Shred the chicken breasts and add to half of the marinade. Set aside.

Clean the shrimp and pat them dry. Mix them with the other half of the marinade in a bowl and refrigerate for 30 minutes.

Heat 4 tbsp oil in a pan and add 1 tbsp shredded ginger. When hot, add the beaten eggs, and when the eggs are partially set, add the rice. Stir-fry for 2 minutes, breaking up the egg with a spatula. Add the soy sauce and chicken stock and keep on stir-frying for 3 minutes. Transfer to a large dish.

Heat 1 cup oil in a pan. Add the shrimp, stirring to separate. Remove and set aside. Add the chicken to the oil, again stirring to separate. Remove and set aside. Cook the peas in 8 tbsp water with 1 tsp salt for 5 minutes. Drain and set aside.

Heat 1 tbsp oil in the pan and add $\frac{1}{2}$ tsp ginger and $\frac{1}{2}$ tsp garlic. When the aroma rises, return the shrimp and peas to the pan. Add the white sauce ingredients and bring to the boil. Pour over one half of the dish of fried rice, using an S-shaped piece of foil to keep the sauce to one side of the dish.

Heat 1 tbsp oil in the pan and add $\frac{1}{2}$ tsp ginger and $\frac{1}{2}$ tsp garlic and when the aroma arises, return the chicken to the pan. Add the red sauce ingredients and bring to the boil. Pour over the fried rice on the other side of the foil. Remove the foil and serve.

CRISPY-COATED CORAL BEAN CURD

14oz fresh shrimp
1½oz pork fat
1 tsp salt
½ tsp pepper
1 tsp sesame oil
2 egg whites
2 tsp cornstarch
7oz bean curd, crushed

Pancakes
2 egg whites

3 tbsp cornstarch

3 cups peanut oil

Sweet-and-sour sauce
4 tsp vinegar
3½ tsp sugar
2 tsp tomato catsup
1 tsp Worcestershire sauce
2 tsp minced red chili
salt to taste

Shell and devein shrimp. Wash them in salt water, drain and pat them dry with a paper towel. Crush the shrimp with the flat side of chopper.

Dice the pork fat into small cubes and put the shrimp, pork fat, salt, pepper, sesame oil, 2 egg whites and the cornstarch into a bowl. Stir the ingredients in one direction until they are sticky, then add the crushed bean curd and continue to stir until well mixed.

To make the pancakes beat the egg whites and add the cornstarch, stirring and mixing thoroughly. Heat a frying pan, rub it with peanut oil and add sufficient egg white and cornstarch mixture to make a wafer-thin pancake. Peel and set aside. Continue until all the pancake mixture is used.

Flatten 1 tsp of the shrimp mixture on the palm of your hand and coat it with a little dry cornstarch. Wrap the mixture in one of the pancakes to form a roll about $1\frac{1}{2} \times 3$in.

Heat the peanut oil and deep fry the rolls at a moderate heat until they are brown.

Serve with sweet-and-sour sauce with minced chili.

CHICKEN IN A NEST

2lb chicken

Marinade
1 tbsp oyster sauce
1 tbsp light soy sauce
1 tsp dark soy sauce
1 tsp sesame oil
1 tsp sugar
1 tsp salt

1 tbsp Chinese yellow wine
2 tbsp cornstarch

4-6 medium black mushrooms
8oz bamboo shoots
1 cup self-raising flour
8 tbsp water
1 tbsp sugar

Cut the chicken into bite-size pieces. Mix together the ingredients for the marinade, add the chicken pieces and set aside.

Soak the black mushrooms in hot water for 30 minutes. Cut off and discard the stems and cut each cap into eight pieces.

Cut the bamboo shoots into slices approximately the same size as the mushroom pieces. Add the black mushrooms and bamboo shoots to the chicken, mix well and set aside.

Put the flour in a mixing bowl, add the water and sugar and mix well. Knead the dough on a lightly floured surface until it is smooth, then leave it to stand for 30 minutes.

Roll the dough into a 'sausage' and divide it into small balls, approximately 1in in diameter. Flatten the ball slightly with the palm of your hand and work it into a bowl shape, about 2in in diameter. Place the bowl on a piece of paper about 2in square and in each bowl or nest put about 2 tbsp of the chicken, black mushroom and bamboo shoot mixture.

Steam the nests for 10 to 15 minutes. Serve.

PORK DUMPLINGS

DIMSUM (*see opposite*)
Rice in lotus leaves surrounded by *dimsum*.
1 Cock's-comb dumplings, 2 Pork liver and shrimp, 3 Pork dumplings, 4 Chicken in a nest, 5 Rice in lotus leaves, 6 Beef and black mushrooms, 7 Shrimp dumplings, 8 Chicken bundles, 9 Squid stuffed with shrimp.

Wrapper
1 cup all-purpose flour
2 eggs
1/4 tsp baking soda

Filling
3 medium black mushrooms
1 1/4lb fillet of pork
4oz pork fat

Marinade
1 tbsp light soy sauce
1/2 tsp sugar
1/2 tsp sesame oil
1/2 tsp pepper
1 tsp Chinese yellow wine
1 tbsp cornstarch
1 egg white
1 tsp salt

Make the wrappers for the dumplings by putting the flour in a mixing bowl. Make a well in the center, add the eggs and baking soda and mix well. Knead the dough on a lightly floured surface until it is smooth.

Roll the dough into a 'sausage', approximately 1 1/2in in

diameter, cover it with a towel and leave to stand for 20 minutes.

Pull the dough apart and roll the pieces between your palms into small balls approximately 1in in diameter. Flatten each ball slightly, dust with flour and roll out into a thin pancake.

Soak the black mushroom in hot water for 30 minutes. Cut off and discard the stems and finely dice the caps.

Cut the fillet of pork and the pork fat into small cubes and mix the pork and mushroom pieces with the marinade ingredients, stirring with a fork until the mixture becomes sticky.

Place one wrapper in the palm of your hand. Put 1 tsp (heaped) of the filling in the center of the wrapper and squeeze the edges gently together until it looks like a change-purse, but leave the top open. If you wish, trim away any excess wrapper, but this is not essential. Continue until all the wrappers are used. Steam over a high heat for 10 to 15 minutes. Serve.

RICE IN LOTUS LEAVES

1½lb long grain rice	*3½oz crab meat*
5oz dried scallops (if dried scallops are too expensive, use dried shrimp)	*2 tbsp chopped ham*
	1 tsp sesame oil
	¼ tsp pepper
10 cups water	*1 tbsp soy sauce*
5oz roast duck	*1 tsp salt*
4oz fresh shrimp	*1 large dried lotus leaf*

Wash and drain the rice. Put the scallops into the water and boil them over a low heat until only about half the water is left.

Put the rice in a large bowl or basin together with the scallop soup and steam the mixture for 15-20 minutes.

Mix the steamed rice and scallops with all the other ingredients and wrap the rice mixture in a large lotus leaf, which has been cleaned by rinsing under boiling water and steamed for another 30 minutes. Secure the lotus-leaf-wrapped parcel with string and place it in a steamer to steam for another 10 minutes.

Serve by bringing the 'parcel' to the table, to be unwrapped on serving.

STEAMED PORK LIVER AND SPARE RIB OF PORK

8oz pork liver	*1 tsp Chinese yellow wine*
1¼lb spare rib of pork	*1 tsp sugar*
	1 tbsp cornstarch
Marinade	
1 tbsp light soy sauce	*1 tbsp ground bean paste*
1 tsp dark soy sauce	*1 tbsp chopped shallot*
1 tsp sesame oil	

Cut the pork liver into slices (⅛in), soak the pieces in water and set aside. Chop the spare rib of pork into bite-size pieces (1½in × 1¾in).

Blend together the ingredients for the marinade and add three-quarters of the mixture to the spare ribs and the remaining quarter to the liver.

Add the bean paste and chopped shallot to the spare ribs and mix well.

Lay the spare ribs in the bottom of small dishes — do not pile it up — and place two or three pieces of liver on top.

Bring 6 pints water to the boil in a large wok with a bamboo steamer in it. Put the small dishes of spare ribs and liver in the steamer, cover and steam over a high heat for 12-15 minutes. Serve.

SQUID STUFFED WITH SHRIMP

4oz dried squid
4oz pork fat
14oz shrimp, shelled and deveined

2 tbsp cornstarch
$\frac{1}{2}$ tsp pepper
$\frac{1}{4}$ tsp salt
1 egg white

Soak the dried squid in hot water for 1 hour before cutting it into pieces $1\frac{1}{2} \times 2\frac{1}{2}$in.

Cut the pork fat into $\frac{1}{8}$in cubes and blanch in boiling water for 2 minutes. Remove and drain.

Pound the shrimp with the flat side of a cleaver and place them in a mixing bowl. Add 1 tbsp cornstarch, the salt and pepper and the egg white to the shrimp and, using a fork, stir in one direction only until the mixture becomes sticky. Add the pork fat and stir until sticky again. Set aside.

Take a piece of squid and dust one side with some of the remaining cornstarch. Place 1 tbsp of the shrimp and pork fat mixture on the floured side of the squid and press gently. Continue until all the squid pieces and shrimp mixture are used.

Arrange the stuffed squid on a plate and steam for 10 minutes over a high heat.

BEEF AND BLACK MUSHROOMS

4oz pork fat
$1\frac{1}{4}$lb ground beef
8 tbsp stock
1 tbsp cornstarch
1 tsp sesame oil

$2\frac{1}{2}$ tsp salt
12 small black mushrooms
1 tsp sugar
1 tbsp peanut oil

Cut the pork fat into tiny cubes ($\frac{1}{8}$in) and blanch the pieces in boiling water for 1 minutes. Rinse under the tap.

Put the ground beef, pork fat, stock, cornstarch, sesame oil and $1\frac{1}{2}$ tsp salt in a mixing bowl and stir, in one direction only, with a fork until the mixture becomes sticky.

Soak the black mushrooms in hot water for 30 minutes, remove and discard the stems and place the caps in a bowl. Add 1 tsp salt, the sugar and peanut oil and mix well. Steam the mushrooms over a medium heat for 5 minutes and set aside.

Divide the beef into 12 portions, molding each portion into an egg shape, and place one mushroom on top of each 'egg'.

Use six small dishes and place two of the beef and mushroom 'eggs' in each dish. Steam over a high heat for 5 minutes and serve.

A WIDE RANGE of *dimsum* is shown here in the bamboo baskets in which they are steamed.
(*Top row, from left to right*) Squid stuffed with shrimp; Steamed pork liver and spare rib of pork; Chicken in a nest; (*center*) Pork dumplings; Chicken bundles; (*bottom row*) Shrimp dumplings; Cock's-comb dumplings; Beef and black mushrooms.

CHICKEN BUNDLES

11oz supreme of chicken   2 tbsp cornstarch
    (preferably with skin on)   4oz roast fillet of pork
2 tsp light soy sauce   3 medium black mushrooms
$\frac{1}{2}$ tsp sugar   2 hard-boiled eggs
$\frac{1}{4}$ tsp sesame oil   8oz Chinese cabbage
$\frac{1}{8}$ tsp pepper

Cut the supreme of chicken into 2 × 1$\frac{1}{2}$in pieces and mix the pieces with the soy sauce, sugar, sesame oil, pepper and corn-starch. Set aside.

Cut the roast fillet of pork into $\frac{1}{2}$in slices and then into 2 × $\frac{1}{2}$in sticks. Set aside.

Soak the black mushrooms in hot water for 30 minutes. Remove and discard the stems and cut the caps into 2 × $\frac{1}{2}$in sticks. Set aside.

Cut each hard-boiled egg into eight pieces and set aside.

Blanch the cabbage in 2 cups boiling salted water for 5 minutes, remove from the water, cut into 4 × $\frac{3}{4}$in strips and set aside.

On each strip of cabbage place some chicken, roast pork and black mushroom pieces and, at the top, near to one end, a piece of egg. Roll the cabbage up to make a neat bundle. Continue with each strip of cabbage until all the ingredients are used.

Put two bundles into each small dish and steam over a high heat for 7-10 minutes. Serve.

SHRIMP DUMPLINGS

Wrapper   1 tbsp lard
see Pork Dumplings (page 110)   1 tsp sesame oil
                                  $\frac{1}{2}$ tsp pepper
Filling   1$\frac{1}{2}$ tsp sugar
1$\frac{1}{2}$lb shrimp, shelled and deveined   2 tsp salt
4oz cooked pork fat
4oz shredded bamboo shoot

Put all ingredients for the filling in a mixing bowl and stir until the mixture becomes sticky. Set aside.

Take one wrapper and place 1 tsp filling in the center. Fold the wrapper up, working with both hands to seal the dumpling. Push the upper edge gently towards the left and make ruffles along the top of the dumpling. Steam the dumplings over a very high heat for 8-10 minutes and serve.

SPRING ROLLS

2 medium black mushrooms
4oz Chinese chives
8oz fillet of pork

Marinade
2 tsp light soy sauce
¼ tsp sesame oil
2 tsp cornstarch
1 tsp Chinese yellow wine

4 tbsp peanut oil
1 tsp chopped ginger
1 tsp chopped garlic
1¼lb bean sprouts
1 tsp salt
20 spring roll wrappers
1 egg white
4 cups peanut oil (to fry spring
  rolls)

Soak the black mushrooms in hot water for 30 minutes. Remove and discard the stems and cut the caps into fine shreds. Set aside.

Cut the Chinese chives into 1¾in lengths. Set aside.

Finely shred the fillet of pork into pieces approximately 2in long. Blend together with ingredients for the marinade and mix with the pork. Set aside.

Heat 2 tbsp oil in a pan and add ½ tsp ginger and ½ tsp garlic. Add the bean sprouts and mushrooms and stir-fry for 2 minutes.

Add the Chinese chives, stir-frying for 30 seconds, add 1 tsp salt, stir and remove from the heat. Set aside.

Heat 2 tbsp oil in the pan and add the remaining ginger and garlic. Add the pork, stir-frying for 1 minute over a medium heat, then increase the heat to very high. Return the bean sprouts, chives and mushrooms to the pan and stir-fry for 30 seconds over a very high heat. Remove, drain and set aside.

On each spring roll wrapper place approximately 3 tbsp bean sprouts and pork. Fold over the side of the wrapper nearest to you and then fold in the ends. Roll the wrapper into a cylinder, wetting the open side with egg white and pressing gently to secure. Repeat with the remaining ingredients to make 20 spring rolls.

Heat 4 cups oil in the pan. Add the spring rolls and fry them over a low heat until they are nicely golden in color, but do not use a high heat.

Serve the spring rolls hot. They may be eaten with Worcestershire sauce to enhance their flavor.

COCK'S-COMB DUMPLINGS

The wrappers are prepared in the same way as for Pork Dumplings (see page 110), but 2 tbsp chopped water chestnut and 1 tbsp chopped coriander are added to the filling. The dumplings are made and cooked as Pork Dumplings.

炸
蝦
丸

炸雪棗

SICHUAN CHICKEN

8-9oz fresh chicken fillet	*6-8 lettuce leaves*
2 tsp shrimp sauce	*1 tsp crushed peppercorns*
½ tsp dark soy sauce	*⅔ tbsp scallion shavings*
1 tsp monosodium glutamate (optional)	*2 dried chili peppers, finely chopped*
1 tsp cornstarch	*3-4 drops sesame oil*
2 cups peanut oil	*1 tsp rice wine*

Slice the chicken fillet into pieces ¼in thick and pound the meat to tenderize it. Mix the chicken with 1 tsp shrimp sauce, ½ tsp dark soy sauce, ½ tsp monosodium glutamate (if used) and 1 tsp cornstarch.

Heat the pan until it is hot and pour 2 tbsp oil into it. Stir-fry the chicken over medium heat until it is almost done (about 1½ minutes). Remove the chicken from the pan to drain.

Stir-fry the lettuce in 4 tbsp very hot oil over high heat and remove immediately from the pan to drain away the oil. Arrange the lettuce around the edge of a plate.

Reheat the pan until very hot and pour in 1 tbsp oil. Stir-fry the crushed peppercorns with the scallion shavings until fragrant, then add the chopped chili followed by the chicken. Add 1 tsp shrimp sauce, ½ tsp monosodium glutamate (if used), the sesame oil and the rice wine. Stir and sauté for a short while over high heat. Remove and place in the center of the plate surrounded by the quick-fried lettuce leaves.

DEEP-FRIED CRAB MEAT BALLS

2 pieces dried bean curd sheet	*1 tbsp chopped leek (white part only)*
8oz shrimp, shelled and deveined	*1 tbsp chopped scallion*
2oz pork fat	*1 tsp salt*
2½oz water chestnuts	*½ tsp pepper*
1 egg white	*4oz crab meat*
2 tbsp cornstarch	*3 cups peanut oil*

COMBINATION STARTERS (*On previous page*) An unusual hot *hors d'oeuvre* from Chiu Chow, a coastal town renowned for its seafood and dipping sauces. Some of these starters are braised or stir-fried, others are coated in batter and deep-fried. They are all presented on the same plate.

Soak the dried bean curd sheets in water until they have softened. Remove and pat dry. Set aside. Chop and mince the shrimps and dice the pork fat and water chestnuts into small pieces.

Place the minced shrimps, the egg white and cornstarch in a mixing bowl and, using a fork, stir in one direction until the mixture becomes sticky and firm. Add the pork and continue stirring until the mixture is thick and firm.

Add the water chestnuts, stirring and mixing well, and then the chopped leek, the chopped scallion, the salt and pepper, and the crab meat, mixing each ingredient in thoroughly.

Place the bean curd sheet on a board. Put the shrimp and crab meat mixture on it, making it into the shape of a thick sausage about 1in in diameter. Roll the bean curd sheet firmly around the mixture, trimming off any excess at the ends.

Place the 'sausage' on a heat-proof platter, and steam it over a high heat for 7 minutes. Remove, set aside and when it has cooled, cut it into 1½in slices.

Heat the oil in a pan. When it is hot, add the crab meat slices. Reduce the heat to low and fry until the bean curd wrapper is nicely golden in color. Serve with Chiu Chow tangerine jam.

Deep-fried shrimp balls and crab balls are often served together, so it is advisable to double the quantity given in the shrimp ball recipes and use half of the shrimp mixture in conjunction with the crab meat dish.

SWEET-AND-SOUR PORK ROLLS

8oz fillet of pork
8oz pork fat
12oz water chestnuts
3oz scallions

Seasonings
1½ tsp five-spice powder
2 tsp salt
2 tsp sugar

1 large piece pork fat

2 tbsp cornstarch, blended with water
3 cups peanut oil
1 tbsp shredded fresh ginger
8 tbsp sweet-and-sour sauce (see page 37)

Garnish
3 pineapple rings, each cut into four pieces

Shred the fillet of pork, pork fat, water chestnuts and scallions and put them in a mixing bowl. Add the seasonings and mix thoroughly.

Flatten the large piece of pork fat on a lightly floured board. Place the shredded mixture on the fat and roll it up to make a sausage 1in in diameter. Trim away any excess fat. Seal the ends with the blended cornstarch and cut the 'sausage' into 1½in sections. Set aside.

Heat the oil in a pan and add the sliced pork rolls. Fry over a high heat for 1 minute, reduce the heat to low and simmer for 4 minutes. Remove and set aside.

Heat 2 tbsp oil in the pan, add the ginger, then add the sweet-and-sour sauce and bring to the boil. Return the sliced pork rolls to the pan and saute for 30 seconds, ensuring that every piece is coated with sauce. Garnish with the pineapple pieces and serve.

煎
蠔
蛋

OYSTER OMELET
Seafood omelets are
typical of Chinese coastal
cooking. This Chiu Chow
version uses the strong
flavor of oysters, which
combines well with egg,
which in this case is
stir-fried.

STEAMED LOBSTER
Steaming lobster
produces a purer taste
than frying, and if ginger
and scallion are used, the
flavor is more delicate
than with other methods
of cooking.

122

梅子鯉魚煲

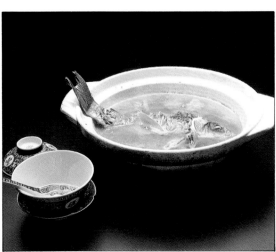

SPARE RIB OF PORK, CARP AND
SALTED PLUM IN A CLAY POT
This is an unusual but
happy combination, the
acidity of the pickled
plum tempering the
richness of the carp and
pork. The surface fat
should be skimmed off
before serving, to leave a
highly flavored clear
broth.

STEAMED EEL WITH PICKLED
PLUM AND SOY BEAN PASTE
Eel, being rich, goes well
with pickled plum. The
addition of bean paste, a
northern speciality, is
unexpected in a dish
from Chiu Chow, which is
just 200 miles from Hong
Kong.

FRIED SHRIMP BALLS

8oz fresh shrimp, shelled
4oz water chestnuts
2oz lean and fat pork (20 per cent
  fat)

Seasonings
1½ tbsp chopped white of leek
1½ tbsp chopped scallion
1 egg

1 tsp salt
½ tsp monosodium glutamate
  (optional)
½ tsp of pepper

½ cup flour
2 cups peanut oil (to fry the shrimp
  balls)

Chop and mince the shrimp and dice the water chestnuts and pork into coarse grains.

Put the shrimp into a bowl and stir until the mixture is sticky. Add the water chestnuts, pork and seasonings and mix well. Add the flour.

Heat the oil in a pan until it is smoking hot. Roll the shrimp mixture into small balls about ¾in in diameter and fry them until they start to turn brown. The mixture makes more than 20 shrimp balls.

Serve with Chiu Chow tangerine jam as a dip.

STEAMED EEL WITH PICKLED PLUM AND SOY BEAN PASTE

2lb freshwater eel
2 tbsp salt
4-6 pickled plums (remove and
  discard the stones)
1 tbsp sugar
2 tbsp soy bean paste

2 tsp dark soy sauce
2 tsp chopped garlic
1-2 tsp red chili, finely shredded
2 tbsp peanut oil
1 tbsp chopped coriander
  (cilantro)

Rub the eel with 2 tbsp salt. Put it in a basin and pour over it approximately 4 cups boiling water. Clean and pat dry. Cut off the back fin, slit the eel open from the back and remove all the bones.

Cut the eel into sections 2in long and place them on large plate.

Mix together the pickled plums, sugar, soy bean paste, dark soy sauce, chopped garlic and finely shredded red chili and spread evenly over the eel. Steam over medium heat for 35 minutes. Pour 2 tbsp very hot (boiling) peanut oil over the fish, sprinkle with the chopped coriander and serve.

The pickled plum brings a special lightness to what might otherwise be a rather heavy dish, while the long steaming time makes the eel melt in the mouth.

OYSTER OMELET

4 medium oysters
1 tbsp cornstarch
4 eggs
2 stems scallions
1 stem coriander (cilantro)

½ tsp sesame oil
1 tsp pepper
1 tsp salt
2 tbsp peanut oil

Clean the oysters, cut them into small pieces (¼in) and mix them with 1 tbsp cornstarch. Set aside.

Beat the eggs together lightly until well mixed. Chop the scallions and coriander into fine shavings and add to the egg.

Blanch the diced oyster in boiling water for 30 seconds. Drain and add the sesame oil, pepper and salt. Mix well.

Heat a pan over medium heat and add 2 tbsp peanut oil. Pour half the egg mixture into the pan and half of the diced oyster. When the edge of the omelet browns slightly turn it over to complete cooking. Repeat with the rest of the egg and diced oyster. Serve on well-heated dish.

SPARE RIB OF PORK, CARP AND SALTED PLUM IN A CLAY POT

1¼lb spare rib of pork
2lb carp or any other freshwater
    fish
3 cups chicken stock

3 cups water
3-4 salted plums
6 slices fresh ginger
2 stalks scallions

Chop the spare rib across the bones into bite-size pieces and blanch them in boiling water for 2 minutes. Remove and set aside.

Clean the carp thoroughly, paying particular attention to the inside of the cavity. Set aside.

Bring the chicken stock and water to the boil in a clay pot. Add all the ingredients and when the mixture boils again, lower the heat to medium. Cook for 5 minutes. Lower the heat further and simmer gently for 15 more minutes. Serve.

STEAMED LOBSTER

2lb fresh or frozen lobster (cooked
    red lobster is not suitable)
6 slices fresh ginger
2oz chicken fat, finely chopped

2 tbsp peanut oil
1 tbsp shrimp sauce
1 tsp Chinese yellow wine
1 tbsp light soy sauce

(Recipe continued on page 128)

鹹菜海鮮湯

PICKLED CABBAGE AND
CHICKEN CLEAR SOUP
Pickled cabbage, known
in China as 'snow pickle',
is used extensively along
the Yangtze River as well
as in Chiu Chow. It gives
the chicken a slightly
vinegary and salty flavor.

126

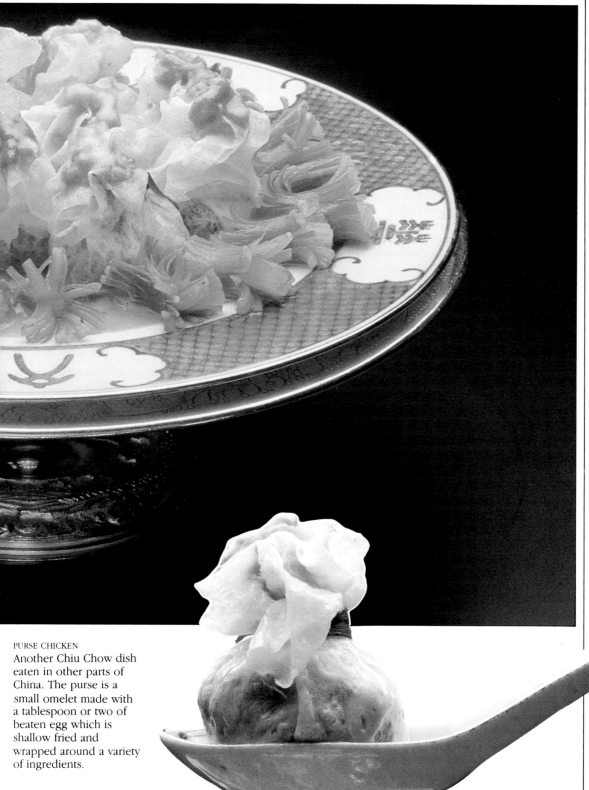

鹹菜海鮮湯

PURSE CHICKEN
Another Chiu Chow dish eaten in other parts of China. The purse is a small omelet made with a tablespoon or two of beaten egg which is shallow fried and wrapped around a variety of ingredients.

Chop the lobster flesh, including the shell, into large bite-size pieces and spread them out on a plate. (Do not pile the pieces in the centre of the plate.) Sprinkle the ginger and chopped chicken fat on top of the lobster pieces.

Bring 5 cups water to the boil in a wok. Place a rack in the wok and put the plate on top of the rack. Steam the lobster over a very high heat for 5-7 minutes. Remove, drain any liquid from the lobster into a bowl and set aside.

Heat 2 tbsp peanut oil in a pan. Add the liquid from the steamed lobster and the shrimp sauce, yellow wine and light soy sauce to make a sauce. Pour over the lobster and serve.

PURSE CHICKEN

9oz broccoli	**Pancakes**
2 medium black mushrooms	3 egg whites
2oz bamboo shoots	2 tsp cornstarch
2oz water chestnuts	3 tbsp chicken stock
1 tbsp salt	
5 tbsp peanut oil	strands of onion
3 scallions	2 tbsp crab roe
5oz chicken breast, diced	
2 tsp egg white	**Sauce**
¼ tsp cornstarch	¾ cup chicken stock
1 tbsp chopped coriander, stem	1 tsp sesame oil
and leaf	2 tsp Chinese yellow wine
	1 tsp salt

Cut the broccoli into shavings, wash in salted water and set aside.

Soak the black mushrooms in hot water for 30 minutes. Remove and discard the stems, finely chop the caps and set aside.

Finely chop the bamboo shoot and water chestnuts and set aside. Bring 1 cup water to the boil, add 1 tbsp salt and 1 tbsp oil and cook the broccoli spears for 5 minutes. Blanch the scallions for 30 seconds. Remove and set aside.

Dice the chicken finely and mix it with 2 tsp of egg white and ½ tsp of cornstarch. Set aside.

Heat 2 tbsp oil in pan. Add the black mushrooms, water chestnut, bamboo shoots, coriander and the chicken mixture. Stir and cook for 1½ minutes over a low heat. Remove, drain and set aside.

Mix together the pancake ingredients. Heat the pan and grease the bottom with oil. Spoon 1 tbsp of the pancake mixture into the centre of pan and make a thin pancake over low heat. Repeat this process until all mixture is used up. (The ingredients given will make approximately 20 pancakes.)

Take one pancake and spoon 1 tbsp of the chicken and vege-table filling into the center, gather up the edges and tie the top of

鹹
菜
海
鮮
湯

the bundle with a strand of onion (use the green part only). Put ½ tsp crab roe on top in the center of the bundle.

Arrange the purses in the center of a plate, sprinkle with broccoli and steam over medium heat for 5 minutes.

Heat 2 tbsp oil in a pan and add the sauce ingredients. Bring the sauce to the boil, stir and pour it over the chicken purses before serving.

PICKLED CABBAGE AND CHICKEN CLEAR SOUP

9oz pickled cabbage	*½ tsp sesame oil*
9oz chicken breasts	*1 tsp cornflour*
Marinade	*4 cups chicken stock*
1 egg white	*1 cup water*
1 tbsp light soy sauce	*4 slices fresh ginger*

Soak the pickled cabbage in 5 cups salted water for 2 hours. Rinse under the tap, squeezing several times and cut into strips ¾ × 3in long.

Cut the chicken breast meat into thin slices 1 × 2 × ¼in. Mix the marinade, add the chicken and set aside.

Put the chicken stock, water, ginger and cabbage in a pot and bring to the boil. Reduce the heat and simmer for 15 minutes.

Bring 2 cups water to the boil. Add the chicken slices, stir to separate and remove immediately. Drain the chicken and transfer the pieces to the soup in the pot. Simmer for a further 3 minutes and serve.

You may prefer to use shrimp, squid and fillet of fish instead of the chicken and make a seafood soup.

DUCKLING AND SALTED LIME CLEAR SOUP

4lb duckling	*1 salted lime*
4 cups chicken stock	*4 slices ginger*

Clean the duck, taking care to remove and discard any excess fat in the cavity and to remove the 'parson's nose'.

Boil 10 cups water and blanch the duck for 5 minutes. Remove and set aside.

Put 4 cups water and the chicken stock into a casserole with a lid. Add the duck, cutting it up if necessary, the salted lime and ginger. Cook in the covered casserole over a low heat for 3-4 hours. Serve.

芥蘭牛丸

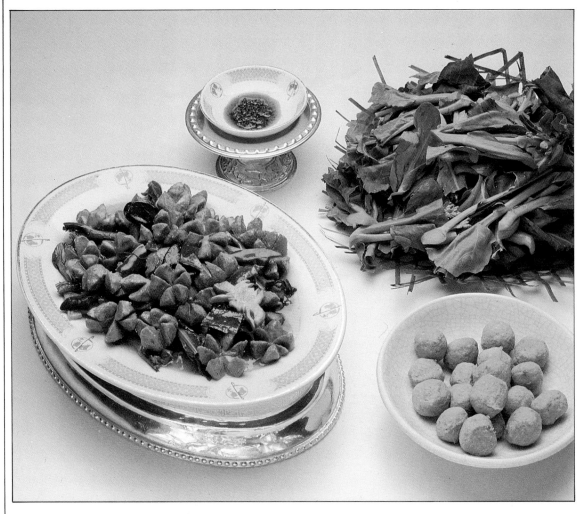

STIR-FRIED BEEF BALLS WITH
DRIED FISH AND CHINESE KALE
Because the meat is
minced, the beef balls
need cooking only briefly.
This recipe calls for
Chinese kale, but spinach
would do equally well.
Sometimes water
chestnuts are used for
crunchiness and the dish
may be flavored with
soy bean paste, sugar and
ginger.

STIR-FRIED GROUND PORK,
CHILI MUSHROOMS AND
BLACK OLIVES
This very unusual
combination of olives and
chili could only occur in
Chiu Chow, which
borders on olive-growing
regions (olives are very
rare in Chinese cooking)
and is also influenced by
the hotness of Sichuan
and Hunan cooking.

雞火砂鍋

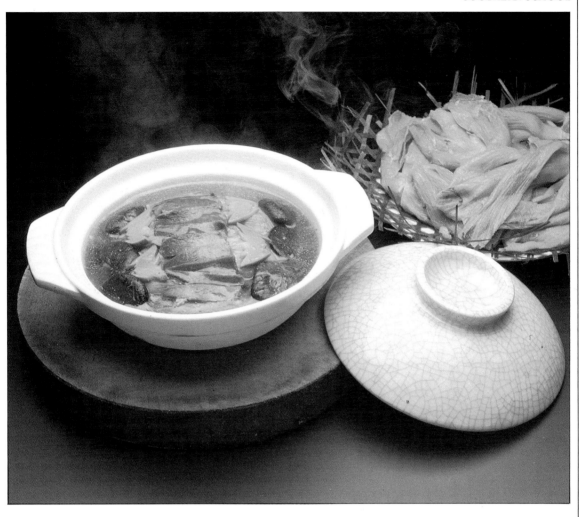

STEWED HAM AND MUSTARD
GREEN IN A CLAY POT
Another Chiu Chow dish
seldom eaten in other
parts of China. The
mustard greens are
slightly vinegary and salty,
which counteracts the
richness of the ham. But
care must be taken during
long cooking that the
dish does not become
too salty.

DUCKLING AND SALTED LIME
CLEAR SOUP
The purpose of the salted
lime is to counteract the
richness of the duckling.
A good deal of fat needs
to be skimmed off the
liquid before serving, but
the flavor is interesting.

STIR-FRIED GROUND PORK, CHILI MUSHROOMS AND BLACK OLIVES

Marinade
1 tsp cornstarch
2 tsp light soy sauce
1 tsp sugar
1 tsp Chinese yellow wine
2 tbsp peanut oil

8oz ground pork

4oz button mushrooms
1 red chili
1 tbsp black olives in sesame oil
*   (black olives for cocktails could*
*   be a good substitute)*
1 tbsp peanut oil
1 tsp chopped garlic

Prepare the marinade and marinate the minced pork. Set aside.

Slice the button mushrooms and finely shred the red chili. Chop the black olives into small pieces.

Heat 1 tbsp oil in pan. Add the garlic and when the aroma arises, add the ground pork. Stir and cook over medium heat for 3 minutes.

Add the black olives, button mushrooms and red chili and stir-fry over medium heat for 2 minutes. This is a wonderful dish to accompany plain cooked rice, rice soup or boiled noodles.

STIR-FRIED BEEF BALLS WITH DRIED FISH AND CHINESE KALE

1¼lb frozen beef balls (see below)
8-12oz dried fish (sole)
1¼lb Chinese kale
8 tbsp peanut oil
1 tsp chopped fresh ginger

4 tbsp chicken stock
1 tbsp fish or shrimp sauce
1 tsp sugar
1 tsp chopped garlic
2 tsp Chinese yellow wine

Defrost the beef balls and rinse them under the tap. Cut about a quarter of the way through each beef ball and set aside.

Remove and discard the bone of the dried fish and break the meat into bite-size pieces. Fry the fish pieces in 8 tbsp oil until nicely browned. Remove, drain and set aside.

Cut the Chinese kale into lengths 1¾ × 2in.

Heat 3 tbsp oil in a pan. Add the ginger and Chinese kale, stir-frying over a very high heat for 1 minute. Add 4 tbsp chicken stock, cover and continue to cook over a very high heat for a further minute.

Uncover the pan and add 1 tbsp fish or shrimp sauce and 1 tsp sugar. Stir rapidly over very high heat for 1 minute.

Add 2 tbsp of oil, the garlic, beef balls and Chinese yellow wine, stir-frying for 2 minutes. Return the fried dried sole to the pan, stir for 30 seconds and serve.

1lb ground beef
1 egg white
4-5 tbsp water
1½ tbsp salt

1½ tbsp cornstarch
½ tbsp sesame oil
½ tsp pepper

If frozen beef balls are not available, you can make your own. Put all the ingredients in a mixing bowl and use a fork to stir — in one direction only — until the mixture becomes sticky and firm. Make up to 20 small meat balls, about ¾in in diameter.

Bring about 4 cups water to the boil, add the beef balls and remove them when they float to the top. Set aside and follow the recipe above.

YIN AND YANG VEGETABLE SOUP

1¼lb spinach leaves
1 tsp baking soda
8oz button mushrooms
4oz chicken breast meat
1 egg white
2 tsp salt

4 tbsp peanut oil
2 tsp Chinese yellow wine
4 cups chicken stock
6 tbsp cornstarch

Blanch the spinach for 2 minutes in 2 cups boiling water with 1 tsp baking soda added. Remove and rinse under the tap for 1 minute. Drain the leaves before chopping them finely. Set aside. Chop the mushrooms finely. Set aside. Finely mince the chicken breast and mix with the egg white and 1 tsp salt. Set aside.

Heat 2 tbsp oil in a pan. Sauté the minced spinach for 3 minutes, add 1 tsp of Chinese yellow wine and 1 tsp of salt and stir together. Add 2 cups chicken stock to the pan having first mixed 3 tbsp of the stock with 3 tbsp cornstarch. Bring the stock to the boil and slowly stir in the cornstarch to make a thick soup.

Place an S-shaped piece of greased cardboard in the center of a soup tureen to divide the bowl into two. Pour the spinach soup into one side of the bowl, holding the cardboard upright by placing a glass of water against it on the empty side.

Heat 2 tbsp oil. Add the mushrooms, sauté for 1 minute and add 1 tsp of Chinese yellow wine. Take 3 tbsp of the remaining stock and mix with 3 tbsp cornstarch. Add the rest of the chicken stock to the pan, bring to the boil and slowly stir in the blended cornstarch. When it boils, stir in the minced chicken and mix well.

Pour the chicken soup into the other half of the soup tureen, first removing the glass of water. Take out the cardboard as gently as possible. The one bowl of soup is then presented and served in the two colors of Yin and Yang.

太極大河素

YIN AND YANG VEGETABLE
SOUP
As with yin and yang rice,
different colors are used
to form the Chinese
symbol of unity in which
positive and negative complement each other.
The green part is usually
made from a green
vegetable. The white part
is also usually vegetable,
perhaps with milk or
chicken added.

SHREDDED PORK, BLACK
MUSHROOMS, CELERY AND
NOODLES IN SESAME SAUCE
The combination of pork,
black mushrooms and
celery is common enough
in China, but what makes
this Chiu Chow dish
unusual is the addition of
a sesame sauce.

芥蘭炒飯

AROMATIC CHIU CHOW RICH FISH SOUP
The Chinese seldom use rice for soup. But this is a thick soup, the consistency of thin porridge, which is eaten for supper or perhaps for breakfast rather than as an accompaniment to other dishes.

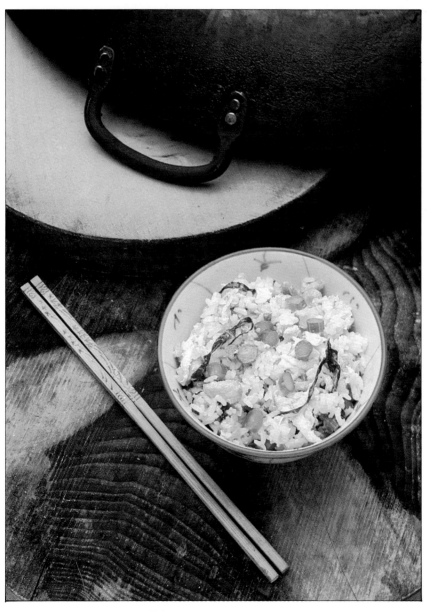

FRIED RICE CHIU CHOW STYLE
Fried rice is a standard Chinese dish but varies from region to region. It nearly always has egg in it. Ham or bacon may be used to give it a sharper, saltier flavor. Seafood can be added, or flaked fish, which produces a dish similar to the English kedgeree.

雞
火
砂
鍋

STEWED HAM AND MUSTARD GREEN IN A CLAY POT

8oz mustard green	**Sauce**
8oz cabbage	1 tbsp oyster sauce
6 medium black mushrooms	1 tbsp light soy sauce
2oz Chinese ham	1 tsp dark soy sauce
1 cup peanut oil	1 tsp sugar
4 slices fresh ginger	1 tsp sesame oil
1 cup chicken stock	2 tsp Chinese yellow wine

Cut the mustard green into pieces 1 × 2in and cut the cabbage into strips the same size.

Soak the mushrooms in hot water for 30 minutes. Remove and discard the stems and cut each cap into half.

Cut the ham into slices $\frac{3}{4} \times 1\frac{3}{4} \times \frac{1}{8}$in.

Heat the oil and fry the cabbage for 1 minute. Drain well and set aside. Fry the mustard green for 1 minute. Drain and set aside.

Heat 2 tbsp oil in a clay pot or casserole and add the mushrooms, cabbage and mustard green. Place the ham on top but do not mix. Add the chicken stock and bring to the boil, reduce the heat and simmer for 30-45 minutes. Add the sauce ingredients and simmer for 2 minutes. Serve in the clay pot or casserole.

SHREDDED PORK, BLACK MUSHROOMS, CELERY AND NOODLES IN SESAME SAUCE

2 oz pork	**Sauce**
1 medium black mushroom	2 tbsp sesame paste
1 Chinese celery	1 tbsp fish sauce or shrimp sauce
4 packets dried egg noodles	1 tsp sugar
2 tbsp peanut oil	1 tsp Chinese yellow wine
	2 tbsp cornstarch
	1 cup chicken stock

Cut the pork into matchstick-size shreds. Soak the black mushroom in hot water for 30 minutes. Remove and discard the stem and chop the cap finely. Set aside. Chop the Chinese celery into small pieces.

Bring 10 cups water to the boil. Add the noodles, stirring to separate, and cook for 3 minutes. Transfer the noodles to a large pan of cold water. Return the noodles to boiling water and cook for 1 minute. Drain and place in a large bowl or on a plate. Set aside.

Heat 2 tbsp peanut oil in a pan. When hot, add the pork and stir-fry for 1 minute over high heat. Add the mushrooms and

芥
蘭
炒
飯

celery, and continue to cook for 30 seconds.

Add the sauce ingredients and bring to the boil. Return the noodles to the pan, stirring, and cook for another 30 seconds.

Transfer the noodles to a serving plate first and place the pork, mushroom and celery on top as a garnish. Pour the sauce over them and serve.

AROMATIC CHIU CHOW RICH FISH SOUP

*5oz fillet of pomfret (sea bream) or
 other white fish*
4oz squid
1 tsp sesame oil
1 tsp salt
1 fillet dried sole

2-3 tbsp peanut oil
2 medium black mushrooms
1 Chinese celery
3 cups chicken stock
8oz plain cooked rice

Cut the fillet of pomfret or whichever white fish you are using into thick slices and cut the squid into bite-size pieces. Mix the fish and squid with 1 tsp of sesame oil and 1 tsp of salt.

Break or chop the fillet of dried sole into tiny pieces and deep fry with 2-3 tbsp oil over low heat until crisp. Drain and set aside.

Soak the black mushrooms in hot water for 30 minutes. Remove and discard the stems and cut the caps into fine shreds. Chop the celery coarsely.

Bring the chicken stock to the boil and add the celery, black mushrooms and rice.

When the soup boils again, add the sliced fish and squid and when it boils again, sprinkle with chopped dried fish and serve.

FRIED RICE CHIU CHOW STYLE

4oz Chinese kale, stem only
4 tbsp peanut oil
2 tbsp shredded fresh ginger
4oz shrimp, shelled and deveined

2 eggs, lightly beaten
8oz cold plain cooked rice
2 tbsp shrimp sauce
¼ cup chicken stock

Dice the stems of the Chinese kale into small pieces.

Heat the oil in a pan and add the shredded ginger, shrimp and Chinese kale, stir-frying them for 1 minute.

Add the eggs (beaten for 10 seconds) and, when they are partly set, add the cold plain rice. Stir-fry over a very high heat. Scramble the eggs, breaking them into tiny pieces with your spoon or spatula.

Add the shrimp sauce and chicken stock and stir-fry over reduced heat for a further 3-5 minutes. Serve.

NORTHERN SCHOOL

BEAR'S PAW served on a gold dish for an Imperial banquet.

(*Opposite page*) FRESHWATER AND SALTWATER shrimps on sale in a fish market.

Peking (or Beijing as it is now called) inevitably acquired a cosmopolitan cuisine as the city attracted cooks from other regions who introduced new dishes into the Peking school of cooking. Chefs came from as far south as Shandong and as far north as Manchuria, Mongolia and Sinkiang, and the presence of the Imperial court inevitably encouraged the development of a wonderful range of rich dishes. As the dynasties changed, the native Han Chinese cuisine was added to under the influence of Mongolian or Manchurian rulers, and now there are more than fifty different styles of cookery in what is known as the Peking school.

In general terms, northern Chinese food, from the Yellow River region around Peking, is more strongly flavored than that of other schools, using a lot of bean paste, garlic and dark soy sauce. While other areas rely on rice as the staple food, northerners favor wheat and plump white dumplings, served steamed, boiled, baked or fried. Wheat noodles are the other main accompaniment or ingredient in a variety of dishes.

Inevitably, in the cool climate in which Peking shivers for six months of the year, 'hot' foods are paramount. Hot pots, the Mongolians' lasting influence, are also popular.

The original hot pot or 'fire kettle', is akin to those found in other northern lands, Korea, Japan and even Switzerland. Like the Mongolian self-service barbecueing griddles, the hot pot is a survivor of prehistoric times. Families or even the whole clan would gather around a massive charcoal-burning stove, as nomadic people everywhere still do. The westerner who has stood around a barbecue pit or camp-fire is part of the same tradition. Even when the Mongolians settled down, their tents becoming permanent homes, the need for warmth and their gregarious natures ensured the modified survival of the central cooking stove. The kitchen was the living room and the cooking range the table.

Meats were marinated, both to preserve them and to add flavors. Further taste was added with piquant sauces into which the griddled or boiled meat slices were dipped. Mutton was preferred to pork, for the nomadic, sheep-herding Mongolians loved their horses and ate their sheep.

Once they had been converted to the new religion, Muslim religious beliefs suited the Mongolians. There are still about four million Chinese Muslims, mostly living in the northern provinces, but all northerners enjoy mutton, unlike southern Chinese, who find the meat's smell unpleasantly heavy.

When the Mongolians conquered Peking their cooking styles came with them. They did not have far to travel as the present border of Inner Mongolia is only about 100 miles north of Peking. The Great Wall of China, the 2,200-year old Chin dynasty line of defence, is just 40 miles north, although part of Peking's Hopei Province extends into the semi-autonomous People's Republic of Inner Mongolia (not to be confused with the Soviet Mongolian

People's Republic further north). Mongolian master-strategist Genghis Khan overcame the Great Wall, and the Mongol Yuan dynasty ruled the Chinese Empire from 1280 when Kublai Khan took the throne. There had been Tartar dynasties before (the Chin and Liao dynasties), but Kublai Khan's reign saw northern conquerors in their full might.

Apart from mutton, the Mongolians brought with them goats and the passion for game meat that was another culinary influence of a nomadic hunting people. In consequence, Chinese game feasts are looked on as northern-style meals and have an exotic appeal even for southern Chinese during their short winters.

Each animal has its special attributes, and through eating the animal, a diner feels he is absorbing those qualities. The consumption of game was another sign of Chinese beliefs in the curative values of food. As usual, sexual prowess was important and gained through deer horns or the penises of a wide variety of wild animals. Generally the game gave the strength and vigor with which northerners survived the rigors of winter.

At the Imperial court there was rarely need for frugality, and game feasts developed into gargantuan, marathon meals. During the rule of the Manchurians (the Ching dynasty) from 1644 to 1911, the Imperial banquet was a culinary orgy that rivalled anything a European renaissance court had prepared. The feasts started out fairly simply in the seventeenth century and were originally served to Emperors when they and their retinues visited southern cities. Less restricted by court protocol, the southern banquets were informal affairs that maintained the traditions of family gatherings. In Peking, however, where the women of the Imperial palaces were forbidden to dine with the men, the style changed.

In their Man (Manchurian) and Han forms the Imperial banquets developed into three-day-long affairs. Bizarre and exotic dishes contrasted with the subtlest recipes collected during southern tours, for the Manchus, recognizing their superior cooking talents, imported cooks from the Yangtze River basin.

Being convinced numerologists, the Chinese insisted that an Imperial banquet should have 365 dishes, just as a famed herbalist had earlier identified 365 valued herbs. No wonder a banquet lasted three days even though the number of dishes was later reduced to 108! It should not be imagined that Imperial courtiers were gourmands rather than gourmets, however. Many of the dishes were prepared for display purposes only at breakfasts and lunches during the three days. The dinners were the main events, offering such exotica as elephant trunks, bear's paws, gorilla lips, camel humps and monkey brains, in an age when wildlife conservation was unheard of.

Today the most popular of the elaborate Imperial dishes is the Peking Duck. Glazed and roasted, the duck should be a specially-reared bird that has been force-fed as generously as a Strasbourg goose. The special pancakes served with the delicately-carved duck skin are one example of the fine flour products of the northern Chinese. Wheat, barley and other grains grew in the Yellow River plains. Rice did not — the climate was too harsh. Bean derivatives were another staple, as were green vegetables, most frequently varieties of Chinese cabbage, such as the one that

THE PAVILION OF FLOATING GREEN in the Imperial Palace, Peking.

honors Peking's nearby city of Tientsin.

Even with a majestic dish like Peking Duck, whose original recipe had 15,000 words, the Chinese abhorrence of waste was apparent. When the duck skin slivers were laid in their little pancakes, the sauce was not the plum variety used everywhere nowadays but a special fermented dough paste made from previous meals' leftover pancakes!

The other famed dish, Beggar's Chicken, which is not of Peking origin, but so popular in Peking restaurants overseas, could have a full book written about it. There are many legends regarding the origin of the clay-baked bird wrapped in a lotus leaf. One illustrates Chinese resourcefulness: it tells how a beggar who had no stove dug a hole in the ground and baked the wrapped chicken over hot ashes. A second legend records that the beggar needed to cook the bird in secret. Both legends admit that the beggar first stole the chicken. Chinese mythologists adore tales in which the rich or powerful are tricked by supposedly simple men! But Beggar's Chicken is certainly not simple. When the clay casing is smashed open and the cooked bird's flavors and aromas waft forth in a cloud of culinary incense, the anonymous beggar deserves to have achieved immortality as a culinary king.

A PEKING vegetable market.

As foreigners and Chinese restaurateurs have discovered, Peking food has various semi-theatrical facets. Noodle-making is one of them. It would be a waste for pasta-masters to hide their skills in a kitchen. In Hong Kong and in some leading Chinese restaurants overseas they are star turns at banquets, as culinary acrobatic jugglers swing and twist one length of dough into incredibly fine strands.

Noodles, pancakes, 'silk thread' bread and heavy *dimsum* pastries filled up a northerner but would not protect an ordinary eater against winter chills. The extensive uses of oils, such as sesame, were one answer, and to balance their extreme tastes and effects, other ingredients — vinegar and salt, garlic and scallions — were incorporated.

Scallions appear in what is one of the Peking school's most representative styles — 'explosive cooking'. Dishes sautéed in wine or vinegar sauce are sizzled with water, coriander, bean paste and with scallions. Another noisy culinary glory of Peking are 'toffee' apples or bananas. The fruits are coated in a toffee-like syrup, which is swiftly dipped into iced water. The syrup solidifies to give crunchy coverings, with glorious results, similar to western toffee-apples, but so much better. Such desserts are typical of all 'Peking' food. Whether it is an hors d'oeuvre, main dish or dessert, a Peking speciality will be tasty, tender and crisp.

The food of Shandong Province is a major element in Peking cuisine. The northern coast of the province has a large number of fisheries, and fish dishes predominate here. Fruit is more plentiful too, and the wines featured in so many Peking dishes are processed from the grapes grown at Chefoo and Tsingtao, the home of the internationally-exported Tsingtao beer, although the main Chinese wine is the yellow rice wine from Zhaoqin (formerly Shaohsing). Shandong is best known for its special stock, made from chicken, duck and pork.

A BEAN CURD FACTORY near Peking run by soldiers of the People's Liberation Army.

There are other regional specialities, but Peking will remain best known for its Mongolian-based reminders of a distant nomadic age of cooking.

北京填鴨

鴨架白菜湯

PEKING DUCK

1 duck (approximately 5-6lb)	40-50 Chinese pancakes (see next recipe)
	6 scallions
Coating	1-2 red chilies
1 tbsp malt sugar, honey or molasses	
1 tsp cornstarch	**Sauce**
½ tsp vinegar	2 tbsp hoisin sauce
	1 tbsp peanut butter
	1 tbsp sesame oil
	1 tbsp Chinese yellow wine

PEKING DUCK (*On previous page*)
Many Chinese dishes are developments from a single ingredient to make maximum use of whatever is available. In this Pekinese selection, economy and variety are combined. The duck carcass, left over from Peking Duck, forms the basis of the soup, while the duck fat is used in the stir-fry to flavor the scrambled eggs. The shredded meat makes good use of meat leftovers, combined with vegetables which abound in all parts of China. The presentation of meat and crispy duck skin together is a play of contrasts between texture and flavor, unified by dipping them in the same sauce.

Clean the duck, removing and discarding any excess fat in the cavity. Tie a piece of string around its neck. Pat dry.

Bring 10 pints water to the boil and turn off the heat. Put the duck into the water and turn it backwards and forwards for about 1 minute. Remove. Bring the water to the boil again and repeat the previous step. Do this twice more (four times in all).

Hang the duck in a cool, drafty place for about 5 hours.

Mix the coating ingredients with 10 tbsp hot water and brush the duck all over with the mixture. Hang to dry for a further 4 hours and apply a second layer of coating.

Preheat the oven to 450°. Put a roasting pan in the oven with a wire rack in it, making sure that there is a space of about 2in between the rack and the pan base.

Place the duck on the rack, breast side up, and roast for 8 minutes. Turn the duck over using a towel — not a fork — and roast for a further 8 minutes.

Reduce the temperature to 350° and turn the duck breast side up again. Roast for 20 minutes. Lower the temperature to 250° and roast for 10 minutes. Increase the heat again to 450° and roast the duck for about 10 minutes. At this point you have to watch carefully to make sure that the skin of the duck does not burn. Turn off the heat once the skin has turned a rich deep red.

While the duck is roasting prepare the Chinese pancakes (see next recipe). Cut the scallions into 2in lengths, shred the tip of each piece and put it in iced water for 10 minutes. Decorate each piece with a red chili ring.

Blend together the sauce ingredients over a low heat. Carve off the skin on the back of the duck. Hold the knife horizontally and carve the skin and meat from the breast and legs, cutting at an angle of 15°. Arrange the skin and meat on a large plate and serve it with pancakes, scallions and the sauce.

Diners help themselves. They place one pancake flat on a plate, put a piece of duck in the center, dip a scallion in the sauce and put it on top of the duck, wrap it up and eat it.

北
京
填
鴨

CHINESE PANCAKES

4 cups all-purpose flour
1½ cups boiling water

1 tbsp sesame oil

Place the unsifted flour in a mixing bowl. Make a well in the center and add the boiling water, stirring rapidly with a fork.

Knead the dough well on a lightly floured surface until it is smooth and firm. Return the dough to the mixing bowl, cover and leave to stand for 1 hour.

Knead the dough briefly on a lightly floured surface and roll into a sausage 1½in in diameter. Pull it apart with your fingers to make about 40 equal-sized pieces. Roll the pieces between your hands to make smooth balls, making sure that they are all the same size.

Lightly oil the fingers and palms of your hands and flatten each ball until it is ¼in thick. Brush the top with sesame oil.

Place one piece of dough on top of another, oiled sides facing, and roll out into a pancake 5-7in across.

Heat the skillet and brush the bottom with sesame oil. Add the paired pancakes to the skillet one at a time. Cook over a medium heat for 30 seconds, turn and cook the other side for 30 seconds.

Pull the paired pancakes apart with your fingers to make two thin pancakes. Place them on a large piece of foil, one on top of the other, oiled side up.

Wrap them in the foil and steam for 30 minutes. Serve as an accompaniment to Peking Duck (see previous recipe). Any pancakes left over can be wrapped in foil and kept in the refrigerator for up to three days.

SCRAMBLED EGGS WITH ROAST DUCK FAT

5-6 tbsp roast duck fat from
    roasting pan of Peking Duck
4 tbsp chicken stock
2 tsp salt

¼ tsp pepper
6 eggs
1 tbsp minced ham
1 tbsp chopped coriander
    (cilantro)

In a mixing bowl mix 2-3 tbsp duck fat with the chicken stock, salt and pepper and the eggs.

Heat 2-3 tbsp of duck fat in a pan and add the egg mixture, beaten and well blended. Scramble over medium heat until set.

Remove and place on plate. Sprinkle with minced ham and chopped coriander and serve.

北京填鴨

PEKING DUCK The duck is carved at table. White gloves are traditional.

A peeling action is used to remove the skin.

The knife is held horizontally.

The juicy meat is kept separate from the crispy skin.

The blade is held at an angle of 15°.

The meat is carved from the breast and legs.

Nothing is wasted.

When there is no more meat to carve, the beak is removed.

北京填鴨

PEKING DUCK
Scallions, cucumber, pancakes and sweet sauce surround the carefully separated skin and meat. Peking duck is eaten in a distinctive way. The diner assembles his own pancakes, with some crispy duck skin, some meat (skin and meat are served separately), some chive or scallion, and a generous dollop of sweet, plummy Peking duck sauce. The whole is then wrapped up. The contrast of textures and tastes is delicious.

Diners prepare their own pancakes.

Cucumber and scallions are dipped in the sauce and placed on the pancake

... together with some duck meat and skin.

The rolled up pancake is ready to eat.

ROAST DUCK BONE, CABBAGE AND MUSHROOM SOUP

1 roast duck carcass (from Peking Duck)
2lb Chinese cabbage
4-6 medium black mushrooms
1 tbsp peanut oil

3 cups chicken stock
4 cups water
3-4 slices fresh ginger
salt and pepper

Chop the duck bones into 3in pieces and cut the Chinese cabbage into 2 × 3in pieces.

Soak the black mushrooms in hot water for 30 minutes. Remove the stems.

Blanch the duck pieces in boiling water for 3 minutes. Remove.

Heat the peanut oil in a pan and stir-fry the Chinese cabbage for 2 minutes. Remove and set aside.

Bring the chicken stock and water to the boil. Add all the ingredients and simmer for 1½ hours. Season with salt and pepper to taste. Serve in a large bowl for diners to help themselves.

STIR-FRIED SHREDDED ROAST DUCK AND BEAN SPROUTS

12oz roast duck meat (from the back of the Peking Duck)
4-6 medium black mushrooms
3 tbsp peanut oil
2 tsp chopped fresh ginger
1½ tsp chopped garlic
1¼lb bean sprouts

Sauce
1 tsp salt
1 tbsp light soy sauce
1 tsp sesame oil
1 tsp sugar
1 tbsp cornstarch
4 tbsp stock
2-3 tbsp peanut oil

1 tsp Chinese yellow wine

Shred the roast duck meat.

Soak the black mushrooms in hot water for 30 minutes. Remove and discard the stems and cut the caps into shreds.

Heat 1 tbsp oil in a pan over high heat and add 1 tsp chopped ginger and ¾ tsp chopped garlic.

Add the bean sprouts, stir-frying over very high heat for 1 minute. Remove and set aside.

Heat 2 tbsp oil in the pan. Add the remaining ginger, garlic and the black mushroom shreds. Stir-fry for 30 seconds, add the roast duck and bean sprouts. Stir-fry briefly. Add the sauce ingredients, and stir rapidly over a very high heat for 30 seconds. Sprinkle with 1 tsp Chinese yellow wine and serve.

烙
韭
菜
盒

PAN-FRIED CHIVE AND DRIED SHRIMP CAKES

1 cup all-purpose flour	1 tsp Chinese yellow wine
6 tbsp cold water	1 tbsp light soy sauce
2oz dried shrimp	2 tbsp shredded fresh ginger
1¼lb Chinese chives	6 tbsp brown vinegar
4 tbsp peanut oil	

Mix the flour and water in a bowl, first stirring with a fork, then kneading with your hands. Transfer the dough to a clean bowl, cover and leave to stand for 45 minutes.

Soak the dried shrimp in 4 tbsp hot water for 30 minutes before mincing them.

Chop the chives and set them aside.

Heat 3 tbsp oil in a pan. Add the shrimp and sauté for 30 seconds, then add the Chinese yellow wine, soy sauce and the chopped chives, stir and cook for 30 seconds. Remove from the pan and set aside.

Knead the dough for about 5 minutes until it is smooth. Roll it into a sausage shape and divide it into approximately 30 portions. Roll each piece into a ball. Flatten the dough with your hands and roll each one into a disc about 2in across.

Put 1 tbsp chives and shrimp in the center of each piece of dough and cover it with another piece. Seal the edges and place it on a lightly floured surface. Cover with a damp cloth. Repeat until all the dough is used up.

Place the cakes on lightly greased plates and steam over a high heat for 15 minutes. Remove and set aside.

Heat the pan and add 1 tbsp oil. Place the cakes in the pan and fry over low heat until golden in color; turn over and fry the other side until golden. Serve with shredded ginger and brown vinegar.

SESAME SHRIMP ON TOAST

1½oz pork fat	1 tbsp chopped coriander
12oz shrimp, shelled and deveined	(cilantro)
2 egg whites	12 slices bread
¼ tsp pepper	1 egg yolk
1½ tsp salt	2 tbsp sesame seeds
4 tbsp cornstarch	2 cups peanut oil

Cook the pork fat in water for 3 minutes and dice it into small pieces.

Crush the shrimp with the flat side of a cleaver and place them in a mixing bowl with the pork fat, 1 egg white, ¼ tsp pepper, 1

烙
韮
菜
盒

PAN-FRIED CHIVE AND DRIED
SHRIMP CAKES
This is a luxury version of
the more standard onion
cakes. The cakes are
actually thickish pancakes
containing chives or
onion and garnished with
shrimp. The dough is
shallow-fried.

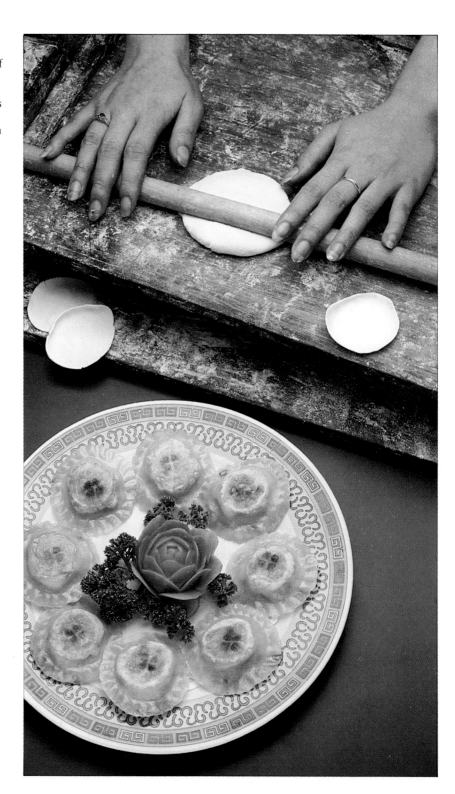

芝
蔴
蝦

SESAME SHRIMP ON TOAST
This dish, usually eaten as a starter, is now quite often served in Chinese restaurants abroad. The shrimp are chopped, spread thickly on bread and deep fried. Sesame seeds are sprinkled on top, and the bread is served in chip-sized pieces.

STIR-FRIED SHRIMP WITH PEAS
Restaurants often put too many peas into this dish, because they are cheaper than shrimp, but it is basically a shrimp dish. Coating the shrimp in a light egg white and cornstarch batter and frying them briefly seals in the juiciness. Tomatoes, which are used here as a garnish, grow in great profusion around Peking in summer.

芝
蔴
蝦

tsp salt and 2 tbsp cornstarch. Stir with a fork, in one direction only, until the mixture becomes consistent and sticky. Add the chopped coriander and stir. Set aside.

Trim the crusts from the bread and cut into slices 1 × 2 × ¼in. Mix 1 egg white with 1 tbsp cornstarch and ½ tsp salt and brush the mixture on top of the bread slices.

Spread the shrimp mixture ½in thick on the brushed side of the bread slices. Sprinkle sesame seeds on top, making sure that every piece is well covered. Mix the egg yolk with 1 tsp cornstarch and brush the bottom of each of the bread slices with the egg mixture.

Heat the oil in a pan. Test the temperature with a thin slice of ginger: when the ginger turns slightly brown, add the shrimp bread, sesame side up. Fry over medium heat for 2 minutes and then turn over. Fry for a further 3 minutes over a lower heat. When nicely browned, turn over, increase the heat back to medium and fry for another 1-2 minutes.

Drain on a paper towel and serve hot.

STIR-FRIED SHRIMP WITH PEAS

1¼lb shrimp	8 tbsp chicken broth
	1 tbsp cornstarch mixed with 3 tbsp
Marinade	chicken stock
1 tsp salt	
1 egg white	2oz peas
1 tsp cornstarch	3 cups peanut oil
	1 tsp salt
Sauce	1 tsp minced fresh ginger
1 tbsp light soy sauce	1 tsp minced garlic
1 tsp sugar	1 tbsp Chinese yellow wine or dry
1 tsp sesame oil	sherry

Shell, devein and thoroughly rinse the shrimp; if they are too big, cut them into halves or thirds. Put the shrimp in a bowl and marinate in the refrigerator in a mixture of 1 tsp salt, 1 egg white and 1 tsp cornstarch for 30 minutes.

Mix together the sauce ingredients, except for the cornstarch.

Blanch the peas in 2 cups water, plus 1 tbsp oil and 1 tsp salt for 2 minutes. Drain.

Heat 2 cups oil, add the shrimp, stirring to separate, drain and set aside.

Heat 2 tbsp oil, add the minced ginger and garlic and when the aroma arises, add the shrimp and peas, stirring rapidly over a high heat.

Thicken the sauce mixture with the blended cornstarch and add it to the pan. Add the yellow wine to the mixture and serve.

京
燒
大
蝦

GRILLED JUMBO SHRIMP PEKING STYLE

2lb jumbo shrimp	*2 tsp sugar*
6 tbsp peanut oil	*1 tsp salt*
6 slices fresh ginger	*4 tbsp chicken stock*
1 tsp garlic	*1 tbsp shredded leek*
2 tbsp Chinese yellow wine	*1 tsp sesame oil*

Trim the jumbo shrimp and devein them. Cut each in half but leave the shells on.

Heat the oil in a pan, add the ginger and garlic and, when the fragrance arises, sauté the jumbo shrimp for 2 minutes. Add the yellow wine, sugar, salt and chicken stock, reduce the heat and cook until the sauce has reduced to about one-third.

Add the shredded leek and the sesame oil and serve.

FISH ROLLS IN WINE SAUCE

1¼lb fillet of grouper or any white fish	*2 tbsp peanut oil*
1 egg white	**Sauce**
1 tsp cornstarch	*1 cup chicken stock*
2 medium black mushrooms	*1 tsp lees of rice wine*
1½oz ham	*2 tsp sugar*
5oz bamboo shoots	*1 tsp salt*
2lb green cabbage	*1 tsp sesame oil*
2 scallions	*2 tbsp Chinese yellow wine*
4-6 slices fresh ginger	*1½ tbsp cornstarch*

Cut the fillet of fish into slices $1\frac{3}{4} \times 3\frac{1}{2} \times \frac{1}{4}$in. Mix the egg white and cornstarch, coat the fillets with the mixture and set them aside.

Soak the black mushrooms in hot water for 30 minutes. Cut off and discard the stems and cut the caps into fine shreds, $1\frac{3}{4}$in long.

Cut the ham and the bamboo shoots into fine shreds, also $1\frac{3}{4}$in long, and blanch the bamboo shoots in boiling water for 1 minute. (If you are using canned bamboo shoots, blanching is not necessary).

Place the shredded bamboo shoots, ham and mushrooms on the fish slices and roll them up. Each roll should have a diameter of $\frac{3}{4}$-$1\frac{1}{2}$in.

Take the heart of the green cabbage and cut it in half. Blanch the cabbage in 5 cups boiling salted water for 2 minutes. Remove and set aside.

Place 2 scallions on a plate. Arrange the fish rolls and

京燒大蝦

GRILLED JUMBO SHRIMP
PEKING STYLE
The name is a little
misleading, because the
shrimp are actually fried.
They are large and juicy
and retain their flavor
well when cooked in this
way. They can be eaten as
a starter or a main dish
and go well with wine.

BRAISED CROAKER IN SOY
SAUCE
Croaker is a meaty fish
common in Hong Kong
and the south-east of
China. It is deep fried a
little before the soy sauce
is added, and ginger and
scallion are often
used as flavorings. It is
good eaten on its own or
with rice.

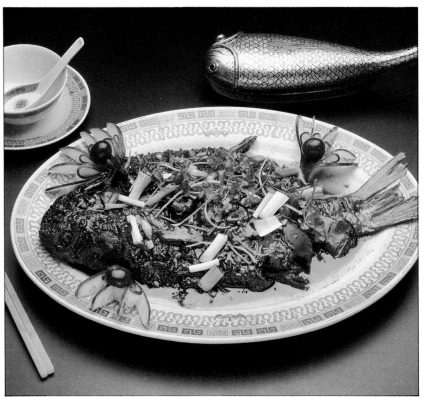

糟溜魚卷

FISH ROLLS IN WINE SAUCE
Sole or plaice is good for this dish. The lightly battered fish is rolled around ham, asparagus or some other filling and poached in hot oil for a very short time before being cooked in wine sauce, sometimes with fish roes. The wine sauce is made from a concentrated wine, sugar and chicken stock.

CRISPY 'SQUIRREL' FISH
When the fish is scored on one side and deep fried, the tail curls up to look like a squirrel's tail. Usually served in sweet-and-sour sauce, this dish is popular in north China and along the Yangtze River.

ginger slices on top and garnish with the poached green cabbage. Steam over a high heat for 5-7 minutes.

Heat 2 tbsp peanut oil in a pan. Add the sauce ingredients, stir and bring to the boil. Pour over the fish rolls and serve.

BRAISED CROAKER IN SOY SAUCE

1½-1¾lb croaker, sea bass, turbot or pike	1 tbsp pork back fat, diced
2 medium black mushrooms	3 tbsp dark soy sauce
8 tbsp peanut oil	1½ tsp sugar
2 scallions	¾cup chicken stock
3 slices fresh ginger	1 tsp sesame oil

Clean the fish thoroughly, pat dry and set it aside.

Soak the mushrooms in hot water for 30 minutes. Remove and discard the stems and cut the caps into shreds.

Heat 6 tbsp oil in a pan. Add the scallions and ginger and remove and discard them when they have browned. Fry the fish for 30 seconds over a very high heat; turn it over and fry the other side for 30 seconds, still over very high heat.

Add the diced pork fat, soy sauce, sugar, chicken stock and black mushrooms to the pan, reduce the temperature and simmer over low heat for 30 minutes. Add 2 tbsp oil to the pan and increase the heat. Reduce the sauce to about half, add the sesame oil and serve.

CRISPY 'SQUIRREL' FISH

3lb croaker or sea bass	½ cup all-purpose flour
	2 cups peanut oil
Marinade	3 scallions (white part only), cut
1 tsp salt	into thin shreds
1 tbsp light soy sauce	1 red chili, finely shredded
1 tsp sugar	1 tbsp shredded fresh ginger
1 tsp Chinese yellow wine	2 cups sweet-and-sour sauce (see p. 37)

Clean the fish. Remove the fillets from both sides, keep the head and tail but discard the backbone. Place the fillets, skin side down, on a chopping-board and score the flesh deeply to form a diamond pattern but do not cut through the skin.

Mix the marinade ingredients together and marinate the fish fillets. Coat the head and tail of the fish with the flour.

Heat the oil and fry the head and tail until nicely golden in color. Remove and set aside. Coat the fillets of fish with the flour and fry over a medium heat until nicely golden. Remove and set aside.

Increase the heat, return the fish to the hot oil and fry for 15 seconds. Remove and drain. Arrange the fish neatly on a serving dish with the head, body and tail in one rounded curve`like a squirrel's tail. Place the scallions, ginger and red chili on top.

Bring the sweet-and-sour sauce to the boil, pour it over the fish and serve.

FISH IN WINE-LEE SAUCE

*1¹/₂lb fillet of white fish such as sea
  bass,cod, turbot or halibut*
¹/₂ egg white
2 tsp cornstarch
*3-4 wood-ear mushrooms
  (champignons chinoises)*
2 cups peanut oil

Sauce
*3 tsp rice wine or 2 tsp wine-lee
  paste if available*
1 tsp salt
1¹/₂ tbsp sugar
1 cup stock

*1 tbsp cornstarch dissolved in 2
  tbsp water*

Cut the fish fillet into six pieces and mix it with the egg white and 2 tsp cornstarch.

Soak the mushrooms in water for 30 minutes and cut them into small pieces.

Heat a pan until it is very hot. Pour in the peanut oil to heat for 20 seconds and add the sliced fish to fry for 15 seconds. Remove and drain away the oil. Add 1 tbsp peanut oil, the sauce, the fish and the mushrooms. Finally add the cornstarch to the pan to thicken the sauce. Serve.

CHICKEN FU-YUNG

4 chicken breasts
4 tbsp chicken stock
6 egg whites
1 tbsp cornstarch
1 tsp salt
1 cup peanut oil
2 slices fresh ginger
1 garlic clove

Sauce
¹/₄ cup chicken stock
¹/₂ tsp salt
1 tbsp cornstarch
2 tsp Chinese yellow wine

2 tsp ham, minced
*2 tsp coriander (cilantro) leaves,
  finely chopped*

Pound the chicken breasts with the back of a cleaver and mince the chicken meat finely. Add 2 tbsp chicken stock to the minced

木須肉

芙蓉雞片

MU HSU PORK
Mu Hsu is a yellow-colored flour, and this is a simple pancake dish that anyone can make. The shredded meat is scrambled with beaten egg and fresh or dried vegetables, including perhaps yellow tiger lily or black mushrooms. The savory mixture is then spooned into a pancake and rolled up.

CHICKEN FU-YUNG
Shredded or minced chicken breast is deep-fried with beaten egg white. The bite-sized pieces are drained then cooked in stock thickened with cornstarch. Wine may be added to the sauce.

FRIED FILLET OF PORK (*Far left*) The use of aromatic pepper in this dish makes it distinctively Pekinese. It is usually served with a dip.

芙
蓉
雞
片

meat and force the mixure through a sieve. Add 1 tbsp egg white to the sieved meat and stir well.

Blend 1 tbsp cornstarch with 2 tbsp chicken stock. Mix the egg whites, salt and minced chicken together, stirring with a fork in one direction only, and add the blended cornstarch, continuing to stir and mix the ingredients thoroughly.

Heat a pan until it is very hot and add the peanut oil. When the oil is warm, add tablespoonfuls of the egg white and minced chicken mixture. Reduce the heat to low and use a spatula to push the egg mixure to and fro in the pan. When it begins to set into snowflake-like pieces, remove them with a perforated spoon, drain and set them aside on a plate to keep warm.

Heat 2 tbsp oil in the pan. Add the ginger and garlic, but remove and discard them when they have turned brown.

Blend together the ingredients for the sauce, add to the pan and bring to the boil. Stir and pour over the egg white mixture.

Sprinkle the minced ham over the sauce and garnish with the chopped coriander leaves before serving.

MU HSU PORK

Seasonings
2 tsp light soy sauce
$1/2$ tsp sesame oil
1 tsp cornstarch
1 tsp Chinese yellow wine

12oz pork
4oz dried tiger lily stems
2oz wood-ear mushrooms
   (champignons chinoises)

2oz bamboo shoots
4 tbsp peanut oil
1 tsp chopped fresh ginger
3 tsp dark soy sauce
2 tsp sugar
6 eggs, lightly beaten
4 tbsp chicken stock
1 tbsp chopped scallion
20 Chinese pancakes (see page
   145)

Blend together the seasonings and add the pork, cut into matchstick-size shreds. Set aside.

Soak the dried tiger lily stems and the wood-ear mushrooms in hot water for 30 minutes. Cut away and discard any tough parts and chop the remainder into $1\frac{1}{2}$in pieces. Thinly slice the bamboo shoots.

Heat 2 tbsp oil in a pan and add the chopped ginger. When the aroma arises, add the pork and cook, stirring, for 1 minute. Add the tiger lily stems, bamboo shoots, wood-ear mushrooms. Add 1 tsp dark soy sauce and 1 tsp of sugar and cook for 1 minute, continuing to stir. Transfer to a plate and set aside.

Heat 2 tbsp oil in the pan and add the lightly beaten eggs, stirring gently with a spatula over medium heat. Cook until set and scrambled. Return the pork and vegetables to the pan and keep on stirring. Break the egg into pieces.

Add the chicken stock, the remaining soy sauce and then the sugar, stirring rapidly over a very high heat for 1 minute, and the chopped scallion. Serve with Chinese pancakes. To eat, place a pancake flat on the plate and spoon Mu Hsu pork on top. Roll up, fold one end over and eat from the open end.

FRIED FILLET OF PORK

Marinade
2 tsp Chinese yellow wine
1 egg white
1 tbsp cornstarch
1 tbsp light soy sauce

1¼lb fillet of pork
1 tbsp salt
1 tbsp Sichuan peppercorns
2 cups peanut oil

Mix together the ingredients for the marinade. Cut the fillet of pork into bite-size slices and marinate for 15-30 minutes.

Sauté the salt and peppercorns over a low heat for 2 minutes. Discard the peppercorns, transfer the salt to a saucer and set it aside for use as a dip.

Heat the oil in a pan until hot. Add the pork and lower the temperature. Simmer for 3 minutes. Turn off the heat and let the pork stand in oil for 5 minutes. Remove and drain.

Heat the oil again until very hot. Return the pork and stir-fry for 1-2 minutes, being careful not to burn it — it should be a nice golden color, slightly crisp outside, but juicy inside.

Serve with peppery salt as dip.

PRECIOUS THINGS CASSEROLE

4-6 medium black mushrooms
4 tbsp peanut oil
3-4 slices fresh ginger
2oz dried shrimp
8oz Chinese cabbage
4 cups chicken stock

2 oz bamboo shoots, sliced
2oz ham
2oz cooked chicken, sliced
2oz cooked shrimp
2oz abalone, sliced
2 tsp salt
1 tsp sesame oil

Soak the mushrooms in hot water for 30 minutes. Remove and discard the stems and set the caps to one side.

Heat the oil in a clay pot. Add the ginger slices, dried shrimp and Chinese cabbage cut into strips ½ × 3in and cook for 2 minutes.

Add the chicken stock, bring to the boil and cook over a medium heat for 10 minutes. Add the sliced bamboo shoot, mushrooms and ham and continue to cook over a medium heat

八寶砂鍋

PRECIOUS THINGS CASSEROLE
A hearty dish that is particularly warming in winter. The ingredients vary but are likely to include dried mushrooms, pork and chicken. Double-boiling makes the liquid very flavorsome.

EXPLOSIVE-FRIED KIDNEY AND TRIPE WITH CORIANDER
This dish calls for careful timing, since overcooked kidney loses its crunch. It is unusual, however, for tripe to be cooked for such as short time.

AROMATIC MUTTON (*Bottom left*)
This is marinated lamb or mutton steamed and cooled then deep-fried until somewhat crisp.

DEEP-FRIED SMOKED SHREDDED CHICKEN (*Bottom right*)
Chicken is smoked on a wire platform in a pot, with rice, sugar and tea leaves at the bottom. The pot is heated and the smoke flavors the chicken.

STIR-FRIED GROUND BEEF WITH SICHUAN PICKLED VEGETABLES (*Opposite page*)
This is the Chinese version of the hamburger. The mustard greens give the beef a salty, vinegary flavor.

榨菜肉末

for 15 minutes. Finally add the cooked chicken, shrimp, abalone, salt and sesame oil. Serve.

If you increase the quantities you can make enough soup to last several meals. However, remember to keep the leftovers refrigerated.

AROMATIC MUTTON

1½lb fillet of mutton	1 tbsp cornstarch
Marinade	12oz leeks
1 tbsp light soy sauce	2 cups peanut oil
1 tsp dark soy sauce	1 tsp chopped garlic
1 tsp sesame oil	1 tsp Chinese yellow wine
2 tsp Chinese yellow wine	

Cut the fillet of mutton into thin slices. Mix together the marinade ingredients, add the mutton slices and set to one side.

Cut the leek into thin slices and set aside.

Heat a pan until it is very hot and add the oil. Heat the oil until it is warm and add the mutton (reserving the marinade in a separate bowl) and stir to separate. Remove, drain and set aside.

Heat 2 tbsp oil in the pan and add the chopped garlic and leek, stir and cook over a very high heat for 1 minute.

Return the mutton to the pan, stirring well. Add the reserved marinade, stirring vigorously over a very high heat for 15 seconds. Finally, add the Chinese yellow wine, stir for another 10 seconds and serve.

EXPLOSIVE-FRIED KIDNEY AND TRIPE WITH CORIANDER

4 pig's kidneys	1 tsp chopped garlic
2 tbsp salt	2oz coriander (cilantro), cut into
2 pieces pork tripe	1½in lengths
2 tbsp cornstarch	1 tbsp soy sauce
8 tbsp chicken stock	1 tsp Chinese yellow wine
2 tbsp peanut oil	1 tsp sesame oil

Split the kidneys in half, remove the membrane and gristle and rub with 1 tbsp salt. Wash them thoroughly and leave them to soak in water for 30 minutes.

Split the tripe, rub it thoroughly with 1 tbsp salt. Wash and rub it vigorously with 2 tbsp cornstarch. Make sure that it is completely clean. Set aside the thick part of the tripe (or you may prefer to cut off the outer skin on both sides). Score the tripe into a diamond pattern and cut it into slices $3/4 \times 13/4 \times 1/4$ in using a cleaver with the blade held at an angle of 25°.

Cut up the kidney in the same way.

Bring the chicken stock to the boil and set it aside.

Heat the oil in a pan and add the garlic, tripe and kidney, stirring over a very high heat for 30 seconds. Add the coriander and hot chicken stock and bring to the boil. Drain off the stock and add the light soy sauce, Chinese yellow wine and sesame oil, stirfrying over a very high heat for 20 seconds. Serve.

Explosive frying involves cooking with very intense heat. It's a technique particularly suitable for ingredients with a delicate texture.

STIR-FRIED GROUND BEEF WITH SICHUAN PICKLED VEGETABLES

2 tbsp peanut oil	2 tbsp chicken stock
2 tsp chopped garlic	1 tsp sugar
1 1/4 lb ground beef	1 tbsp Chinese yellow wine
5oz Sichuan pickled vegetable, minced	

Heat 2 tbsp oil in a pan and add the garlic. When the aroma arises, add the ground beef, stirring over a high heat for 30 seconds.

Add the minced pickled vegetable and continue to stir and cook until the ingredients are dry. Add the stock, sugar and Chinese yellow wine to the pan and stir vigorously over a very high heat for 30 seconds. Transfer to a plate and serve with Sesame Cakes (see recipe below).

SESAME CAKES

4 cups all-purpose flour	1 tsp yeast
2/3 cup lard	1 tbsp sesame oil
4 tbsp water	2 tbsp sesame seeds

Use a fork to mix half of the flour and lard with the water and yeast. Knead with your hands until the dough is smooth, cover and leave to stand for 30 minutes.

Make a second dough with the remaining flour and lard, again kneading with your hands until the dough is smooth. Set it aside.

Roll the first dough into a sausage shape and divide it into

乾
燒
二
鬆

DEEP-FRIED CONPOY AND SHREDDED KALE

This dish is often called Crispy Seaweed and is a great favorite in Chinese restaurants in the west. The kale is cut into fine shavings which are double deep fried until they are very crispy. These are sprinkled with crispy deep-fried and shredded conpoy (dried scallops), which provide an evocative suggestion of the sea.

PAN-FRIED ASPARAGUS IN EGG BATTER

The asparagus is fried in a small amount of oil with a little chicken stock added to allow longer cooking time for the stalks. Flavored oil or chicken fat with garlic and ginger may be used, but any stronger seasoning will detract from the subtle flavor of the asparagus.

SHARK'S FIN, HAM AND
CABBAGE SOUP
The emphasis here is on
the purity of the shark's
fin, which will already
have been through
several stages of cooking
before it reaches the clay
pot with the cabbage and
ham. The humble
cabbage makes a curious
contrast to the shark's fin,
a relatively luxurious item.

砂鍋魚翅

approximately 24 pieces. Roll each piece into a ball. Repeat with the second dough, rolling it into a sausage and dividing it into approximately 24 pieces. Roll the pieces into balls but work them into cup shapes with your fingers. Put a ball made with the first dough inside each cup and wrap the cup around to form a large ball.

Roll the ball into a sausage between your palms and then use a rolling pin to roll each sausage into a long oval. Brush the top with oil.

Lay one oval on top of another, oiled sides facing, and press them together around the edges. Coat the top with sesame seeds and bake for 15-20 minutes at 350°.

To serve, cut the baked sesame cakes across the middle into two pouched pieces. Minced beef with pickled vegetables is spooned into the open ends of the cakes (or pouches) and they are eaten as a kind of sandwich.

DEEP-FRIED SMOKED SHREDDED CHICKEN

1¼lb chicken breasts	**Marinade**
1 tbsp tea leaves	1 tbsp soya paste
2 tsp sugar	1 tsp light soy sauce
1 tbsp cooked rice	1 tsp Chinese yellow wine
	½ tsp salt
	2 tbsp all-purpose flour
	2 cups peanut oil

Steam the chicken breasts for 15 minutes. Heat a smoking pan and place in it the tea leaves, sugar and rice. Fit a rack into the pan and place the chicken on top. Cover the pan and when the pan is full of smoke, smoke the chicken for 5 minutes over medium heat.

Cut the chicken into strips ⅛ × ⅛ × 2in and mix the chicken pieces with the marinade. Take the meat out of the marinade and coat the strips with flour. Save the marinade.

Heat the oil in a pan and deep fry the chicken over medium heat until nicely golden. Take care when frying the chicken: turn off the heat immediately if you think the oil is getting too hot. Remove the chicken and drain.

Reheat the pan and return the chicken. Add the remaining marinade to the pan, stirring vigorously over a high heat, and serve.

If you use cooked chicken there is no need to steam the meat before smoking. In fact, cooked chicken is recommended since raw chicken seldom gives the crispiness that is one of the beauties of this lovely dish.

鍋
塌
露
笋

PAN-FRIED ASPARAGUS IN EGG BATTER

3 tbsp peanut oil
1¼lb asparagus
1 cup chicken stock
1 tsp salt

2 eggs, lightly beaten
1 tbsp all-purpose flour
1 tsp Chinese yellow wine

Heat 1 tbsp oil. Add the asparagus (using only the tender spears), two-thirds of the chicken stock and the salt. Cook over a low heat until all the stock has evaporated and set aside.

Mix the eggs with the flour in mixing bowl and thoroughly coat each asparagus spear with the egg batter.

Heat 2 tbsp oil in the pan, reduce the heat and arrange the asparagus, one by one, in the pan. Sauté gently for 1½ minutes. Turn the asparagus over and sauté for another 1½ minutes.

Add the remaining chicken stock, sauté until all the stock has evaporated and add the Chinese yellow wine. Sauté for 30 seconds and serve.

DEEP-FRIED CONPOY AND SHREDDED KALE

4oz conpoy (dried scallops)
2 slices fresh ginger
1 tsp Chinese yellow wine
5oz Chinese kale leaves or pickled
snow cabbage leaves

2 cups peanut oil
2 tsp sugar
1 tsp salt

Soak the conpoy in water for 30 minutes. Add the ginger and Chinese yellow wine and steam for 15 minutes. Remove the conpoy, tear it into fine shreds and pat dry. Set it aside.

Cut the Chinese kale leaves into fine shreds, pat it dry and set aside. (If you are using pickled snow cabbage, soak it in 5 cups hot water for 30 minutes. Change the water and soak for another 30 minutes. Squeeze it dry, tear the leaves into small pieces and set them aside.)

Heat the peanut oil in a pan. Add the conpoy, stirring to separate, and fry until nicely golden in color. Remove, pat dry with paper towels and set aside.

Add the kale or cabbage, again stirring to separate, and fry for 1 minute. Remove. If the vegetable is not crispy enough return it to pan for a short time. Remove and pat dry with paper towels.

Sprinkle 2 tsp sugar and 1 tsp salt over the vegetables and mix well. (If you are using pickled snow cabbage, there is no need to add salt.) Place the crispy vegetables on a plate, arrange the conpoy on top and serve.

涮羊肉

涮羊肉

MONGOLIAN HOT-POT
The essence of this dish is a very rich stock which is made by dipping bundles of thinly sliced lamb into boiling water or stock. The meat is eaten as it is cooked, each person making up his own dipping sauce from a selection. When the meat is finished, the stock, with cabbage and noodles added, is drunk from the dip bowls.

TOFFEE APPLES
Small pieces of apple are coated in batter and deep fried. They are then coated again in molten rice sugar and quickly dipped in iced water so that the coating becomes cold and brittle, while the apple inside remains hot.

SHARK'S FIN, HAM AND CABBAGE SOUP

1½lb dried shark's fin (skin and bone removed)	6 medium black mushrooms
2 scallions	6 tbsp peanut oil
2oz fresh ginger	6 slices fresh ginger
1½lb spare rib of pork	1½lb cabbage
8 cups chicken stock	4oz ham, sliced

Prepare the shark's fin according to the recipe for Shark's Fin Consommé on page 40.

Bring 4 pints water to the boil. Add the scallions, 2oz ginger and the shark's fin and simmer for 2 hours. Remove the shark's fin and set it aside.

Blanch the spare rib of pork in 5 cups boiling water for 5 minutes. Rinse under the tap.

Bring the chicken stock and 4 cups water to the boil. Add the spare rib of pork, simmer for 2 hours and set aside.

Soak the black mushrooms in hot water for 30 minutes. Cut off and discard the stems.

Heat the oil in a clay pot and add the ginger slices and cabbage, cut into strips ½ × 3in, stir and add the shark's fin. Place the mushrooms and ham slices on top, add the stock and bring to the boil.

Simmer for 1 hour and serve.

MONGOLIAN HOT POT

2lb lamb	shrimp sauce
4 cakes bean curd	soy sauce
4-6 Chinese dried mushrooms	Chinese yellow wine
1¼lb cabbage	wine vinegar
1¼lb spinach	sugar
9oz bean-flour transparent noodles	chili oil
	fermented bean curd cheese
	1 bundle chopped chives
Sauce	chopped coriander (cilantro) leaves
sesame oil	4 stalks chopped scallions
sesame paste	

Cut the lamb into wafer-thin slices and arrange the slices on a large platter (or on several smaller plates to avoid stacking up slices of lamb). Cut each cake of bean curd into eight or ten pieces.

Put plenty of water into the pot. Add the mushrooms and bring to the boil.

涮
羊
肉

Diners are encouraged to mix their own sauce. One recipe would be to mix 1 tbsp each of sesame oil and sesame paste with 1 tsp each of shrimp sauce, light soy sauce, Chinese yellow wine and wine vinegar and ½ tsp sugar.

The more adventurous might care to add 1 tsp each of chili oil and fermented bean curd cheese and chopped chives and stir in chopped coriander and scallion.

Mix the sauce in a bowl, sample it and correct it to taste.

Pick up one or two slices of lamb at a time with chopsticks or put them in a small, long-handled wire basket, designed especially for this purpose. Cook the lamb very briefly in the boiling water in the hot pot. Transfer to the sauce bowl and eat.

Add the vegetables and bean curd half way through, and the bean-flour noodles towards the end, when the boiling water has turned into a rich soup after all the meat has been cooked in it. The contents of the hot pot should then be spooned or ladled out into the individual diner's bowl and drunk as a soup.

TOFFEE APPLES

3 apples
1 tbsp lemon juice
½ cup cornstarch
2 tbsp sesame seeds
1 cup ice cubes

3 cups iced water
2 cups peanut oil
½ cup sugar
1 tsp vinegar

Peel and core the apples and cut each into six pieces. Cut each piece into three. Sprinkle lemon juice over the apples immediately to prevent discoloration. Coat the apple pieces with cornstarch and set them aside.

Sauté the sesame seeds in a pan over a low heat. Set aside.

Rub a serving plate with oil and set it aside. Place the ice cubes and iced water in a bowl and set them aside.

Heat the oil and fry the apple for 10 minutes until nicely golden. Remove, drain and set aside.

In another pan bring 1½ cups water to a vigorous boil. Add the sugar, stirring until it starts to caramelize, then add the vinegar and stir.

Add the apple pieces until they are evenly coated with syrup. Sprinkle sesame seeds over the apple and transfer them to a serving plate.

Dip the syrup-coated apple pieces into the iced water. Remove immediately or when the syrup hardens and becomes brittle. It is worth practising this recipe a few times to achieve the correct contrast between the brittle, ice-cold coating of caramelized sugar and the hot, tender apple center.

WESTERN SCHOOL

South-western China's Sichuan Province is the most heavily populated region in China. Set about by high mountains, it stays warm in winter and gets very hot in the summer. The province's quarter of a million square miles of mostly mountainous territory rise in the west to the lofty Tibetan plateau. A land of mountains and mists, Sichuan is nevertheless a fruitful region, for the Yangtze River runs across it, and the heart of the province is the Red Basin. In its rich lands both the people and the farms are fertile — the population density is very high and the crops include rice, maize, sugar-cane, beans and tobacco.

Ancient irrigation systems and intense cultivation ensure that three crops of rice can be harvested annually. The irrigation schemes, which channel the converging waters of four rivers, are one indication of the independent power that the Sichuanese once had. Many marvellous Buddhist ruins and monuments are further evidence of what was, until fairly recently, a proud kingdom.

Virtually inaccessible, because of those mountan ranges, Sichuan was not brought into contact with the outside, northern Chinese world until the reign of Kublai Khan in the thirteenth century, and local rulers maintained more than titular control for many centuries after. Thus Sichuan cuisine is quite distinct from other Chinese regional cooking schools. It can be divided into two basic types. The food of the peasants, in the countryside of the Red Basin, is the type the outside world now knows best. It is hot and fiery, heavily spiced with chili, truly thrilling fare. Good, home-cooking style Sichuan food will have peppery, hot chili-laden dishes, which, nevertheless, can never be confused with westernized Indian food, with its lashings of curry powder. Home-style Sichuan food can have a great subtlety and variety of fiery flavors.

The other main Sichuan cooking style arose among the ruling class and reflected external Chinese influences. Less hotly spiced, Sichuan banquet dishes are even subtler pleasures.

The province's geographical isolation from the rest of China did not mean that it was cut off from the outside world. In many ways Sichuan looked south for its culinary influences, and its fiery accent is part of a widespread culinary language that developed

BAMBOO SHOOTS, one of Sichuan's treasures (opposite).

KUNMING LAKE, Yunnan Province (middle).

A HOUSE IN CHENGDU is surrounded by bamboo groves (below).

TEA-PICKING in the Puer region of Yunnan, near the Burmese border. This strong black tea is considered good for a hangover.

all the way from India, through Burma and Thailand and across to Indo-China. Indeed, the people of Sichuan are related to their southern neighbours both racially and culturally. The Thais, for instance, are generally believed to have originated in this south-western region of China, moving south from Sichuan and its southern provincial neighbour of Yunnan. Even now there is a major Thai-speaking tribe living in the Sichuan region, along with sizeable populations of other minorities that are also found in Thailand and Indo-China's hill-tribe areas.

Buddhism was brought north from India two thousand years ago. Traders soon followed the missionaries, as they have in any religious movement, bringing with them both the spices and the cooking concepts of India. Spices and herbs were adopted both as medicines and cooking ingredients.

There are many theories why Sichuan Province has used chilies more than other areas in China. One story claims that the chili was the only crop easily grown in the isolated mountain communities and was therefore used to help preserve foodstuffs. There may be some truth in the story, but it does not explain why the whole region, including its most fertile areas, adopted the chili with such alacrity. It is more likely that the chili proved its value as an antidote to the region's high humidity, for humidity tends to dull the appetite. Chili not only stimulates the appetite, it increases the ability of the palate to appreciate various tastes.

Do not imagine that a Sichuan chili is anything like a normal capsicum. Sichuan's glorious little chilies are culinary fire-bombs, which the Sichuanese fry to increase their explosiveness.

But, as in classic Indian cuisine, a cook does not rely on just one spice. His stock of taste enhancers and appetite stimulators includes brown peppercorns, ginger, garlic and onions. Sichuan cuisine, in fact, is famous for its refined and meticulous cooking styles and seasoning methods, which can create a palate-exciting variation of tastes within a single dish.

'Fish aroma' dishes are special delights. The 'fish aroma' is a special sauce flavored with vinegar, wine lees, garlic, ginger, pepper, scallion and the ever-faithful broad-bean paste. There is no trace of fish in the sauce.

Another outstanding Sichuan flavor is equally wrongly named. It is called 'queer taste'. But don't be misled by the name for there is nothing queer about dishes flavored with it. The sauce is a perfect blend of a Sichuan cook's five key flavors — sweet, sour, salty, peppery and, of course, chilied. 'Queer taste chicken' is an especially famous dish, best enjoyed with spirits.

Other elements in a Sichuan dish include bitter flavors and distinctive aromatic and fragrant qualities. Sichuan cuisine places much less emphasis on side sauces: each dish is designed to provide its own textural and taste contrasts. Stir-fried dishes are cooked to the point where juices are almost entirely reduced .

Smoked duck is a Sichuan speciality. Even a connoisseur has difficulty in identifying a dominant factor, for the duck is seasoned with a variety of ingredients — ginger, orange peel, cinnamon, peppercorns and coriander — and then marinated in Chinese rice wine. After an initial steaming, the duck is smoked over a charcoal fire sprinkled with chips of camphor wood and red-tea leaves. The bird's final flavor and aroma are a heavenly blend of fascinating contrasts.

MAO TAI, the spirit made from the grain of these sorghum plants, is 110° proof, stronger than pure Russian vodka. It is a speciality of Guizhou.

Sichuan food also incorporates dishes adopted from the neighbouring provinces of Hupei, Hunan and Yunnan, the last of which is particularly famed for its ham. However, each province has distinct characteristics. Yunnan is the odd man out among the Indo-Chinese areas because Kublai Khan's successors deliberately settled many Muslim Mongolians in the border territory. Just as the 'colonies' of Han Chinese had previously taken Peking practices out into the provinces, so did the Muslims in Yunnan.

Back to Sichuan for a momentary vote of thanks to the ubiquitous bean curd. The protein-rich soya bean features in many regional cuisines, and some of its finest versions can be found in Sichuan fare. The long Buddhist influence explains the Sichuan glories, but it is not necessary to be a vegetarian to appreciate the splendid versatility of bean curd in all its forms, whether it is as soft as an egg custard, cake-like, dried or frozen.

One seventeenth-century Chinese gentleman considered that one piece of advice about bean curd had to be passed on to his son. So he put it in his will, charging the son to remember that dried bean curd should be eaten with fried peanuts to savor the taste of the finest ham. Another writer claimed that good bean curd was a finer experience than bird's nest (a rare treat).

The same writer also sang the praises of bamboo shoots, another of Sichuan's treasures. Bamboo is one dish that must be prepared without any potentially overwhelming companions, and enjoyed by itself with just a trace of flavor from pickled vegetable or dried shrimp roe. The poet Su Shih wrote that he would prefer to take a meal without meat rather than live in a place without bamboos. 'Without meat a man can grow thin', he noted. 'Without bamboo he will grow vulgar', he added.

However, understanding the subtlety of Sichuan food is not that simple. It is China's boldest food and perhaps the only one that shows off external non-Chinese influences. Proudly different from mainstream Chinese cooking styles, it recalls an age of Sichuan independence.

醉
雞

BRAISED CROAKER

BRAISED CROAKER IN CHILI SAUCE

The fish is deep fried then cooked in a chili sauce made from fresh or dried chilies and soy sauce. Browned pork with ginger and scallions are used to intensify the flavor.

SHRIMP IN SICHUAN SAUCE

The shrimp are fried then cooked with other ingredients such as bamboo shoots or diced eggplant in a pre-mixed hot sauce which consists of chopped chili and garlic in soy paste. Wine and sugar can also be added.

酸辣湯

SOUR AND PEPPERY SOUP
Usually called
hot-and-sour soup, this is
popular everywhere. A
strong savory soup stock
is made adding fresh
chicken or shrimp and
chopped bean curd. Then
a thickened sauce with
pepper, soy sauce and
plenty of vinegar is
combined with the stock.

**SICHUAN DUMPLINGS IN RED
SAUCE**
The dumplings are made
by steaming or poaching
minced pork wrapped in
a thin skin of dough. The
sauce is actually red oil
made by soaking dried
chili peppers in oil
overnight.

BRAISED CROAKER IN CHILI SAUCE

1½-1¾lb croaker, sea bass, turbot or pike
2 tbsp cornstarch
10 tbsp peanut oil
2 tsp chopped garlic
1 tbsp chopped scallion
1 red chili (cut into small rings)

1 tbsp chili broad bean paste (flat bean paste)
1 tbsp soy bean paste
1 tsp vinegar
1 tsp sugar
1 cup chicken stock
2 tsp Chinese yellow wine
1 tbsp chopped coriander (cilantro)

Clean the fish thoroughly, pat it dry and lightly coat with cornflour. Heat 8 tbsp oil in pan. Fry the fish over a very high heat for 2 minutes on each side. Remove and set aside.

Heat 2 tbsp of oil in pan. Add garlic, scallion and chili, and stir.

Add chili broad bean paste, soy bean paste, vinegar and sugar, stirring. When the aroma rises, add chicken stock. Stir to mix well. Return fish to pan, cover it up, and cook over medium heat for approximately 10 minutes.

Add 2 tbsp of oil around the edge of the fish. Increase heat, and add Chinese yellow wine. Garnish with coriander and serve.

JUMBO SHRIMP IN SICHUAN SAUCE

1¼lb jumbo shrimp, trimmed and deveined
3½ tbsp peanut oil
2 tsp yellow wine
2 tbsp chicken stock
1 tbsp Sichuan hot bean paste
½ tbsp chopped Sichuan pickle

2 tsp chopped fresh ginger
1 tsp salt
large pinch chopped scallion
8 tbsp chicken broth
1 tbsp tomato sauce
½ tsp chili oil or sauce

Cut each shrimp into three equal parts. Heat the pan for 10 seconds and add 2 tbsp oil. Stir-fry the shrimp in the hot oil for 1 minute over a high heat. Add the wine and chicken stock, cover and allow to cook for 1 minute. Remove from heat.

Heat 1½ tbsp peanut oil in a pan. Add the bean paste, pickle, ginger, salt, scallion and chicken broth. Stir together for 30 seconds. Add the shrimp and continue to stir-fry over moderate heat for 1 minute. Add the tomato sauce and chili oil or sauce and stir-fry once more over high heat. Serve.

SOUR AND PEPPERY SOUP

¾oz black mushrooms
1½oz chicken blood pudding

¾oz sea cucumber
¾oz cooked chicken or ham
¾oz squid

1½oz bean curd
¾oz cooked pork
1 tsp light soy sauce
1 tsp dark soy sauce
1 tsp pepper
1 tsp chili oil
3 cups chicken stock

2 tbsp cornstarch, blended with 2
    tbsp water
1 egg, lightly beaten
2 tsp chopped scallion
2 tsp brown vinegar
1 tsp sesame oil

Soak the black mushrooms in hot water for 30 minutes; remove and discard the stems and cut the caps into shreds.

Shred the blood pudding, sea cucumber, chicken meat (or ham), squid, bean curd and cooked pork, and add to the soy sauces, pepper and chili oil in a pan. Add the shredded mushroom and the chicken stock and bring to the boil. Stir in the softened cornstarch and the egg.

Place the scallions, brown vinegar and sesame oil in a soup tureen, pour the soup into the tureen and serve.

SICHUAN DUMPLINGS IN RED SAUCE

4 medium black mushrooms
8oz fillet of pork
4oz pork fat
4oz chives or white of scallions
2 egg whites
2 tbsp cornstarch
1 tsp salt
1 tsp sesame oil
40 wonton wrappers

Red sauce
2 tbsp sesame oil
1 tbsp chili oil
1 tbsp chopped garlic
1 tsp Sichuan peppercorn powder
2 tbsp sesame paste
2 tbsp dark soy sauce
1 tbsp chopped young leek or
    scallion
2 tsp sugar

Soak the black mushrooms in hot water for 30 minutes. Remove and discard the stems. Set aside.

Finely dice the fillet of pork and the pork fat and chop the chives or the white of the scallions into tiny pieces.

Place the pork, mushrooms and chives in a mixing bowl. Add 1 egg white, 1 tbsp cornstarch, 1 tsp salt and 1 tsp sesame oil and mix well.

Put 1 tbsp of the pork mixture in the center of a wonton wrapper. Mix the other egg white with 1 tsp cornstarch and wet two of the edges of the wrapper. Fold up the wrapper diagonally to form a triangle and press the edges to seal. Fold two opposite corners over and stick together with more of the egg white and cornstarch mixture.

In a large pan boil 8 pints water and add the dumplings. When they float to the surface, add 1 cup cold water and bring back to the boil again. Remove and drain the dumplings, arranging them in a medium-size serving bowl (six dumplings to each bowl). Prepare the red sauce and serve.

肝
蒸
湯

CHICKEN LIVER MOUSSE CLEAR
SOUP
Either chopped chicken
liver or chicken blood
can be used. It is steamed
until set then chopped
into diamond-shaped or
triangular pieces which
are added to the soup
during cooking. For a
livelier taste, chili can be
added either to the livers
beforehand or to the
soup itself.

STIR-FRIED CHICKEN KUNG-PO
STYLE
Chicken is diced into
cubes, coated in cornstarch
and stir-fried, first in very
hot oil, then with the oil
drained off. Kung-po style
means the dish is
colored pink with a
combination of soy sauce
and red oil, which gives it
a distinctive flavor and
appearance.

MULTI-FLAVORED CHICKEN

The particular flavor of this dish comes from the addition of sesame sauce to the sauce during cooking.

川椒鷄球

SMOKED DUCK SICHUAN STYLE

Smoke from sugar and tea burned together permeates the previously braised duck meat to flavor it. The whole duck is placed on a wire rack in a pot with a lid and the mixture is heated inside the pot until it smokes. After cooling, the duck can be deep fried and eaten with a dipping sauce.

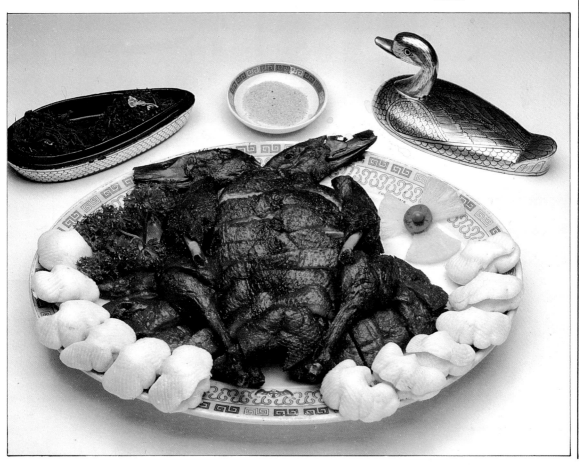

宫
保
雞
丁

STIR-FRIED CHICKEN KUNG-PO STYLE

1¼lb breast of chicken

Seasoning
1 tsp sugar
1 tbsp dark soy sauce
1 tbsp cornstarch

Sauce
1 tsp sugar
2 tsp vinegar
1 tbsp dark soy sauce
3 tbsp stock

2 tsp cornstarch

4 tbsp peanut oil
1 tsp peppercorns
1 tsp dried red chili, cut in ring form
1 tsp Chinese yellow wine or dry sherry
3 slices ginger
1 tsp chopped garlic
2 tsp chopped scallion
4oz roasted peanuts

Cut the chicken into cubes (½in) and mix the meat with the seasoning ingredients.

In a separate bowl, blend together the ingredients for the sauce and set it to one side.

Heat the oil in a pan add the peppercorns and dried red chili and when the chili darkens in color, pour the oil into a bowl through a strainer. Discard the peppercorns.

Return the oil and the dried red chili to the pan, and add the chicken. Stir-fry for 1 minute, add the yellow wine, then the ginger, garlic and scallion. Keep on stirring and turning the ingredients. Add the sauce ingredients, stir well, then add the roast peanuts. Stir and serve.

A variation of this spicy, full-flavored dish is given in the recipe below.

CHICKEN WITH SICHUAN CHILI

14oz breast of chicken
2 tsp shrimp sauce
1 tsp dark soy sauce
1 tsp cornstarch
3½ tsp Chinese yellow rice wine or sherry
2 cups peanut oil
1½oz pearl leaves (finely shredded

leaves of Chinese kale or mint are a good substitute)
1 tsp chopped scallion
½ tsp Sichuan peppercorns
½ tsp monosodium glutamate (optional)
3-4 drops sesame oil

Cut the chicken into slices ¼in thick and pound the meat to tenderize it. Mix the chicken with 1 tsp shrimp sauce, 1 tsp dark soy sauce, 1 tsp cornstarch and 1½ tsp rice wine.

Heat a pan until it is very hot and add the oil. When hot, fry the chicken until it is almost cooked but do not let the oil boil. Remove the chicken from the pan to drain.

Fry the vegetable leaves in hot oil over a high heat for 75

seconds. Remove them from the pan, drain thoroughly and arrange them around the edge of a plate to keep warm.

Heat the pan again until it is very hot. Add 1 tbsp oil. Fry the scallion until fragrant, add the peppercorns and then the chicken. Add 1 tsp shrimp sauce, ½ tsp monosodium glutamate (if used), 3-4 drops sesame oil and 2 tsp rice wine and sauté for a short while over high heat. Remove and place in the center of the plate surrounded by the stir-fried vegetable.

CHICKEN LIVER MOUSSE CLEAR SOUP

8oz chicken liver	1 tsp salt
5 egg whites	2 tsp Chinese yellow wine
1 egg yolk	¼ tsp pepper
4 cups chicken stock	½ tsp sesame oil

Finely mince the chicken livers and run them through a sieve.

Add the 5 egg whites and the egg yolk to 1¼ cups chicken stock. Stir to mix well together in a bowl. Add the salt, Chinese yellow wine, pepper and sesame oil, stir and blend together thoroughly.

Grease the bottom of a medium-sized soup tureen and transfer the mixture to it to steam over medium heat until set, which will take 7-8 minutes.

Heat the remaining chicken stock and place it in a large soup tureen. Transfer the chicken liver mousse to the large tureen, taking care not to damage the mousse in the transfer. Serve for eating throughout the meal.

SMOKED DUCK SICHUAN STYLE

2lb duck	½ tsp pepper powder
1½ tsp peppercorns	2 tbsp Chinese yellow wine or dry
2 tbsp salt	sherry
2 tbsp jasmine tea	4 cups peanut oil
1 tbsp sugar	1 tbsp sesame oil

Clean the duck and soak it in 10 pints water with peppercorns and salt added for 4 hours.

Blanch the duck in boiling water for 5 minutes. Dry thoroughly.

Heat a dry pan over moderate heat, add 2 tbsp jasmine tea, 1 tbsp sugar and cover with a lid. After 1 minute, place a wire rack in the pan and lay the duck on the rack. Replace the lid firmly and

回
鍋
肉

DOUBLE-COOKED PORK

A very popular dish that is easy to prepare. Belly of pork is usually preferred by the Chinese, as it has more fat. The meat is boiled, sliced and cooked again in a hot savory sauce thickened with red oil or tomato paste, which gives it a pleasing color and taste.

SLICED PORK WITH GARLIC SAUCE

This Sichuan dish is also very popular in Peking, where garlic is used liberally. Its appeal lies in its simplicity. Boiled belly or shoulder of pork is sliced very thinly then sprinkled with minced garlic, by itself or stirred into a light soy sauce.

芹黄牛肉麵

GROUND BEEF, CELERY, CHIVES
AND NOODLES IN SOUP
The proper name for this
typical Sichuan dish is
Dan-Da noodles. It
consists of noodles in a
clear stock with stir-fried
beef in a savory sauce
placed on top so that the
flavor and hotness
permeate the noodles and
liquid.

smoke the duck for about 10 minutes over low heat and then leave to stand in the smoke until it turns light golden brown.

Rub the duck all over with pepper powder and Chinese yellow wine and steam for 2 hours. Set aside.

Heat 4 cups peanut oil in a deep pan. When hot, add the duck and deep fry until the skin is rich golden brown in color and crispy.

Take the duck out of the pan and brush with sesame oil. Chop into bite-size pieces and serve.

MULTI-FLAVORED CHICKEN

4-5lb fresh chicken	*1 tbsp chili sauce*
	1 tbsp chopped garlic
Sauce	*1 tsp ground peppercorns*
2 tbsp sesame oil	*3 tbsp shredded scallions*
1 tsp brown vinegar	*1½ tsp salt*
1 tsp sugar	*8 tbsp stock*

Clean the chicken thoroughly.

Put 6 cups water into a pan and bring to the boil. Add the chicken and simmer for 10 minutes over low heat. Remove the chicken and rinse under the tap for 2 minutes. Return the chicken to the water and boil for a further 5 minutes. Rinse with cold water again.

Remove the bones from the chicken and hand-shred the meat, arranging the shredded chicken on a plate.

Blend together the ingredients for the sauce. Pour it over the chicken on the dish and serve.

SLICED PORK WITH GARLIC SAUCE

2 stalks scallions	*1 tsp chopped scallions*
6 slices fresh ginger	*1 tbsp dark soy sauce*
1¼lb shoulder of pork	*4 tbsp chicken stock*
2 tbsp peanut oil	*1 tsp sesame oil*
1 tsp Sichuan peppercorns	*1 tsp sugar*
1 tbsp chopped garlic	*1 tsp chili oil*

Bring 10 cups water to the boil. Add one of the scallions and the ginger and pork and cook for 30 minutes. Remove the pork from the pan and rinse it under the tap. Return it to the water and cook over medium heat for another 30 minutes.

Take out the pork again, rinse it under the tap, pat dry and cut into wafer-thin slices. Arrange on a plate and set aside.

Heat 2 tbsp oil in a pan and add the peppercorns. When they change color, take them out of the pan and discard. Add the garlic and remaining scallion stalk (cut into ½in sections) and sauté for 15 seconds. Add all the other ingredients, stir and mix well. Pour the mixture into a bowl and serve the pork with this sauce so that diners may dip the slices of meat in it.

A simple but tasty cold cut. An excellent starter to alert your palate for more exciting spicy dishes to follow.

DOUBLE-COOKED PORK

1¼lb belly of pork
4 tbsp peanut oil
1 tsp salt
1 tbsp chili bean paste or Sichuan tou pan jiang

1 tbsp yellow bean paste
2 tsp dark soy sauce
4oz garlic leaves, cut into 2in lengths

Cook the pork in 3 cups boiling water for 20 minutes. Rinse the meat for 1 minute under the tap and then cut it into slices 2 × 1½ × ¼in.

Heat the oil in a pan over medium heat, add the pork slices and stir-fry for 10 seconds. Add the salt and continue to stir until the pork pieces curl up.

Add the chili bean paste and the yellow bean paste and continue to stir. Finally, add the soy sauce and garlic leaves. Stir-fry for 10 seconds and serve.

GROUND BEEF, CELERY, CHIVES AND NOODLES IN SOUP

8oz Chinese celery
8oz Chinese white chives or the white part of leeks
1¼lb dried white wheat flour thick noodles
2¼ cups chicken stock, boiling
4 tbsp peanut oil

1¼lb ground beef
2 tsp chopped scallion
2 tsp chopped fresh ginger
2 tsp chopped Sichuan pickle
1 tbsp dark soy sauce
2 tsp chili oil
2 tsp Sichuan peppercorn powder
4 tbsp chicken stock

Chop the celery and white chives or leeks into shavings. Set aside.

Bring 10 cups water to the boil and add the noodles. Reduce the heat to medium and cook for 5-6 minutes. Transfer the noodles to a large pan of cold water, stirring to keep them separate. Drain the noodles and return them to a pan of boiling

DRY-FRIED CRISPY BEEF

乾煸牛肉絲

DRY-FRIED CRISPY BEEF

The long frying time of the Sichuan dry frying technique means that the beef is really dry and crisp, providing a pleasant contrast of texture to rice and other ingredients such as scallions.

DRY-FRIED BEEF, FLAVORED WITH AGED ORANGE PEEL

The beef can be prepared in two ways, either stewed or crisp fried with sauce. Either way, the flavor comes from shredded orange or tangerine peel.

SESAME BEEF

Sesame seeds, used extensively in Sichuan cooking, are heated in a dry pan to bring out their aromatic flavor and added to dry-fried minced beef. Chili is often added too.

乾煸牛肉絲

芹黄牛肉麺

water and cook for a further 2 minutes. Test with your fingers to see if they are cooked: they should be firm but also soft and easy to break. When they are cooked remove and drain them and divide them among four or six bowls.

Add 2 cups of boiling chicken stock to the noodles in the bowls.

Heat the oil in a pan, add the ground beef and stir-fry quickly over high heat. Add the chopped celery and chives and, continuing to stir, cook for 30 seconds.

Add the remaining ingredients, including an additional 4 tbsp chicken stock, stir and bring the contents to the boil. Ladle over each bowl of noodles and serve one bowl to each diner.

DRY-FRIED BEEF, FLAVORED WITH AGED ORANGE PEEL

1¹/₂lb lean beef (round, tenderloin, etc.)	3 cups peanut oil
1 dried, aged orange or tangerine peel	¹/₂ tsp salt
	1¹/₂ tbsp sugar
3 slices fresh ginger	1¹/₂ tbsp dark soy sauce
2 green chili peppers	1 tbsp hoisin sauce
2 dried red chili peppers	2 tbsp good stock
2 stalks scallion	2 tbsp Shaohsing rice wine or dry
6 tbsp cornstarch	sherry
1 egg, lightly beaten	1¹/₂ tsp sesame oil

Shred the beef into pieces the size of a 'double matchstick'. Wash and drain the pieces thoroughly.

Soak the dried orange or tangerine peel in warm water for 20 minutes and cut it into matchstick-size shreds. Cut the ginger and the green and red chili peppers into similar size pieces and the scallion into 2in sections.

Mix together the cornstarch and lightly beaten egg and coat the shredded beef, making sure that each piece is evenly covered.

Heat the oil in a pan or wok and, when a crumb dropped into the oil will sizzle, add the beef. Using a fork or wooden chopstick to separate the shreds, stir-fry the beef over a medium heat for 6-7 minutes. Remove the beef from the pan with a perforated spoon and set it aside to drain. Meanwhile, allow the oil in the pan to increase in temperature until it is smoking. Return the beef and stir-fry for a further 2 minutes. Remove the beef with a perforated spoon and drain thoroughly.

In a separate pan or wok heat 3 tbsp oil. When the oil is hot, add the shredded ginger, orange or tangerine peel and green and red chili peppers and the scallion pieces. Stir-fry them together for 1 minute before adding the salt, sugar, soy sauce, hoisin sauce, stock and wine. Continue to stir and cook for another minute, by which time the liquid should have reduced by about half. Return the beef to the pan and stir well to mix the ingredients together for 1 minute. Sprinkle the sesame oil over the mixture and serve.

SESAME BEEF

12oz sirloin steak

Marinade
1 tbsp light soy sauce
1 tsp dark soy sauce
1 tsp sugar

1 tsp sesame oil
1 tsp Chinese yellow wine

1 tbsp white sesame seeds
3 cups peanut oil

Cut the steak into thin slices $1\frac{1}{2} \times 2 \times \frac{1}{8}$in. Prepare the marinade and mix the beef slices with it. Set it to one side.

Sauté the sesame seeds in a pan over a low heat until they are nicely golden in color. Set aside.

Heat the peanut oil. Add the beef, reduce the heat to medium and fry for 3 minutes. Remove the meat and bring the oil back to a high temperature. Return the beef to the oil and fry for a further 30 seconds.

Drain the beef and pat it with a paper towel before transferring it to a serving dish. Sprinkle it with sesame seeds and serve.

DRY-FRIED CRISPY BEEF

1lb sirloin steak
4oz carrot
1 Chinese celery
4 tbsp peanut oil
3 tsp Chinese yellow wine

Seasoning
2 tsp chili bean paste
1 tbsp hoisin sauce

2 tsp chopped garlic
2 tsp chopped scallion
1 tsp sesame oil
1 tsp salt

1 tbsp sugar
1 tbsp chopped scallion
1 tsp chopped fresh ginger
$\frac{1}{2}$ tsp Sichuan peppercorn powder

Cutting across the grain, thinly slice the beef and then further cut it into $\frac{1}{8}$in shreds. Set aside.

Cut the carrot and celery into similar tiny pieces and set aside.

Heat a pan until it is very hot and add the oil. When the oil is hot, add the beef, stirring gently to separate, and 2 tsp Chinese yellow wine. Keep on stirring until the beef shreds are 'bouncing' in the pan.

DRY-FRIED FRENCH BEANS
Highly savory pure
vegetable dishes — such
as this Sichuan specialty —
are often used as a
contrast to a pure meat
dish in the composition of
a well-balanced meal.

**SHREDDED EGGPLANT IN FISH-
FLAVOR SAUCE**
This full-flavored and
somewhat spicy dish is
excellent with rice,
especially in the absence
of a substantial meat dish.

SICHUAN BRAISED BEAN CURD
This is a very well known
Sichuan dish which is now
extremely popular all over
China — and is also a
great favorite in Japan! It
should be served with
rice, either plain boiled
rice, or rice stir-fried with
egg.

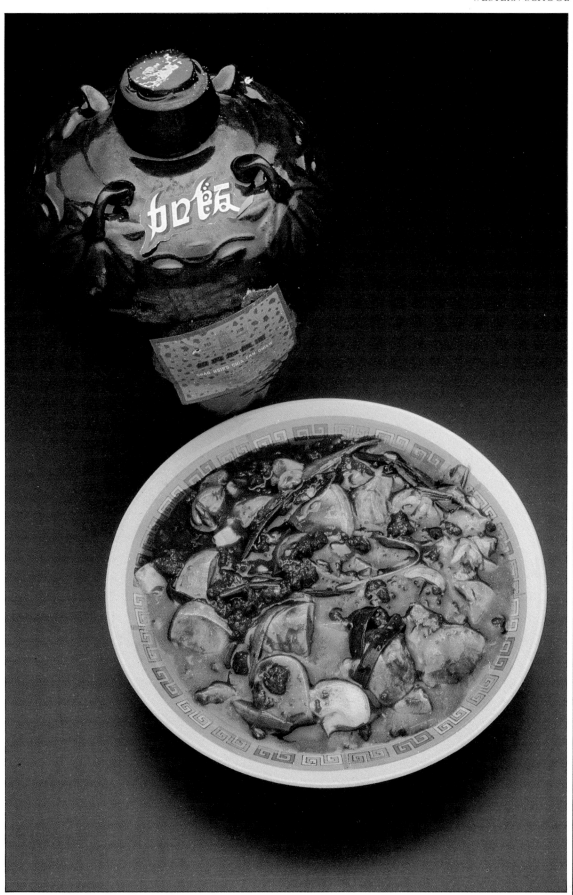

七彩銀芽

Thoroughly mix together the seasonings and add them to the beef. Stir-fry over a high heat for 45 seconds. Add 1 tbsp sugar and 1 tsp Chinese yellow wine. Stir-fry for 15 seconds.

Add the celery and carrot, stir-fry for 30 seconds before adding the ginger, scallion and peppercorn powder. Stir and serve.

The dry-frying method is an unique contribution to Chinese cuisine developed by Sichuan chefs. Beer, rather than wine, is the best accompaniment to this particular dish.

DRY-FRIED FRENCH BEANS

12oz French (thin, green) beans
1 dried red chili
1 cup peanut oil
1 tbsp chopped garlic
1 tsp chopped fresh ginger
1 tbsp chopped dried shrimp

Seasoning
2 tsp rice wine

1 tsp monosodium glutamate
*   (optional)*
¹/₂ tsp salt
1 tsp sugar

2 tsp dark soy sauce
¹/₄ cup water
¹/₂ tsp sesame oil
1 tsp vinegar

Trim the beans and cut each one in half. Chop the chili into small pieces.

Heat the pan until it is very hot. Add the peanut oil. Fry the French beans and remove after 30 seconds. Drain the oil away.

Heat 1 tbsp oil in pan, add the chopped garlic, ginger and dried shrimp and stir-fry until fragrant (about 30 seconds). Add the seasonings and French beans to the pan and sauté for a further 30 seconds.

Add the soy sauce and water and simmer over low heat until the sauce has almost evaporated.

Add the sesame oil and vinegar and sauté for a short while longer over high heat. Serve.

SHREDDED EGGPLANT IN FISH-FLAVOR SAUCE

1¹/₄lb eggplants
1 red chili
¹/₂ stalk of celery
1 stalk of coriander (cilantro)
2 stalks of scallions
2 cups peanut oil
2 tsp chopped garlic
1 tsp chili and bean paste
2 tsp rice wine lees or Chinese
*   yellow wine*

1 tsp chopped fresh ginger
¹/₄ cup good stock

Seasoning
¹/₂tsp salt
1 tsp monosodium glutamate
*   (optional)*
1¹/₂ tsp wine vinegar
2 tsp chili sauce

Peel the eggplants and cut them into thin slices.

Cut the chili, celery and coriander into ½in slices and the scallions into shavings.

Heat the pan until it is very hot. Add the oil and, when the oil begins to smoke, add the eggplants. Fry for 30 seconds. Remove the eggplants as soon as they start to turn brown and drain away the oil.

Heat the pan again until it is very hot and pour 2 tbsp oil into it. Add the chopped chili, celery and coriander together with the chopped garlic, chili and bean paste, rice wine and chopped ginger and stir-fry until fragrant. Add the stock and then the seasonings.

Put in the sliced eggplants and cook over high heat until most of the liquid is gone. Remove and place on a plate. Sprinkle with the chopped scallions and serve.

This vegetable dish is delicious with plain cooked rice. 'Fish-flavor', a Sichuan speciality, is unique to Chinese cuisine. There are several explanations as to why it is so called (it certainly *doesn't* taste of fish!). The most convincing is that it was originally used for fish dishes.

SICHUAN BRAISED BEAN CURD

4 tbsp peanut oil
2oz ground beef
1 tbsp chili broad bean paste
1 tsp chopped garlic
1 tbsp chili oil
½ tsp chili powder
2 tsp dark soy sauce
4 cakes bean curd (approximately 12 oz)

4 tbsp chicken stock
2 tsp cornstarch, softened in 2 tsp water
1 tbsp chopped scallion
1¼ tsp Sichuan peppercorn powder
2 tsp Chinese yellow wine

Heat the oil in a pan, add the ground beef and chili broad bean paste and cook for 30 seconds, stirring continuously. Add the chopped garlic, chili oil, chili powder and soy sauce, stir-fry and cook for 1 minute. Chop the bean curd into ½in cubes and add to the pan together with the chicken stock, stirring and mixing all the time. When the contents boil, reduce the heat and simmer for 5 minutes.

Stir in the blended cornstarch and add the chopped scallion and peppercorn powder. Stir in the wine and serve.

This is perhaps the best known Sichuan dish outside the province, and extremely popular in overseas Chinese restaurants. It is excellent with rice or bread — whether Chinese steamed bread or a hard-crust French loaf.

EASTERN SCHOOL

CRABS FROM SHANGHAI are sold at market tied with sea grass.

(*Opposite page*) A TRADITIONAL SHANGHAI tea-house built on a lake.

Of all China's regional cuisines, that of Shanghai is the most diverse. Not surprisingly, for the region covers three major East China Sea coastal provinces — Kiangsu, Chekiang and Fukien — and the two inland provinces of Anhwei and Kiangsi. The southernmost of the coastal provinces, Fukien, has its own distinctive styles of cooking, its isolated communities having over a hundred different dialects and almost as many culinary peculiarities. In the Yangtze delta area, dominated by the city of Shanghai, many famous cities have contributed major dishes and techniques to what we broadly label Shanghai food.

Two geographical features ensured that the Shanghai region would be rich both economically and in culinary terms. First, the coastline, which extends from Fukien in the south through Chekiang Province, up to Kiangsu Province. Seafood in many forms is an eastern region joy. Second, the Yangtze, Asia's longest and China's most important commercial river, is a 3,400-mile lifeline. Networks of irrigation canals running from it increased the fertility of the Yangtze valley, as in Sichuan. In the river estuary itself is a cluster of famous cities — Suzhou, Hangzhou, Yangzhou, Nanking — as well as Shanghai itself. On the Yung River estuary south of Shanghai lies Ningpo, one of the original treaty ports.

First let us look at Shanghai, China's largest city. The independent municipality in south-east Kiangsu Province has 12 million inhabitants, who live in a city that is often compared with Hong Kong, for Shanghai was only a glorified fishing village until the middle of the nineteenth century. The Treaty of Nanking (1842) opened it and other coastal ports to foreign trade. The rest is history, as they say, but old Shanghai, the original community outside the Foreign Concessions, did have its own cuisine, and that native Shanghainese culinary tradition still defines the basic outlines of Shanghai food. Generally it is more greasy, sugary and strongly flavored than food from other regions, and stewing, frying and braising are its principal cooking techniques. As usual, climatic considerations seem to have caused the characteristics.

Shanghai winters tend to be cold. As in northern China, bread, dumplings and noodles, particularly plump noodles, were favored, as was oil. In contrast, the summers were warmer, usually uncomfortably hot. Soya bean products were the customary Chinese response to the human need for cooling food. Preserved foods were essential ingredients, preserved vegetables, fish, shrimp, mushrooms are Shanghainese specialties. The 100-day-old egg is a famed Shanghai favorite.

Any saltiness in the preserved ingredients was balanced by other flavorings, and sugar was a frequent additive to meat dishes (as in Korea). Perhaps understandably, native Shanghainese food has never been considered sophisticated enough to be served at elegant banquets, that honor having been reserved for Peking and Cantonese food.

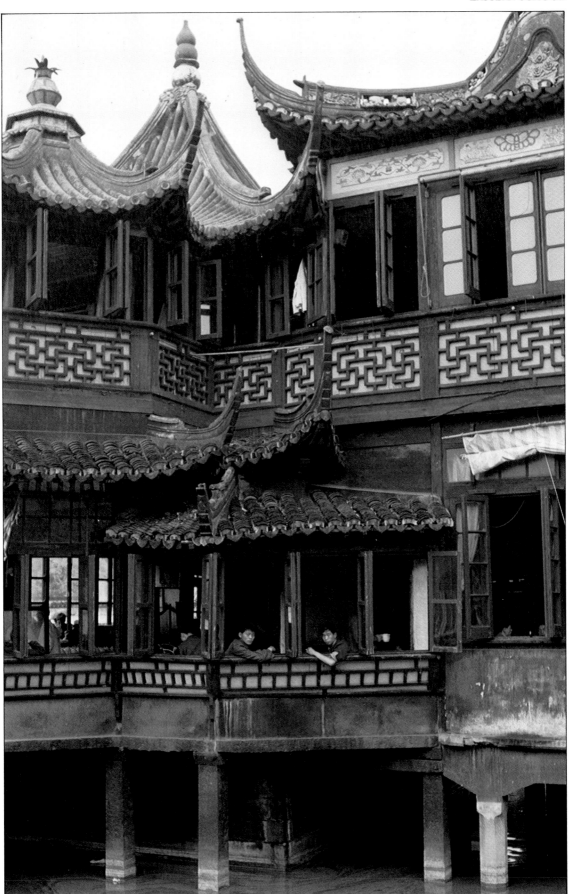

In the nineteenth century, however, Shanghai became China's most cosmopolitan city. Pictures of the famed riverside Bund reveal the foreign architectural influences that overwhelmed the seaport, but they cannot show the various cultural and culinary influences, both from outside and also from within China, that created the Shanghainese love of good food and dining out.

The port of Ningpo, an older trading center, gave the region's cuisine its saltiness. Salt and preserved ingredients are strongly featured in Ningpo dishes, and the steamed and fish dishes, which were also highly developed in Ningpo, contributed several renowned dishes to the Shanghai repertoire. Two examples are braised turtle in sweet brown sauce and yellow fish in soup.

Hangzhou is deservedly famous. During the later Sung dynasty it was the capital of south China and famed for its silk. Marco Polo thought it the 'finest and most splendid city in the world'. He wrote with mouth-watering approval of its 'abundance of victuals', its 'plump and tasty' lake fish, and its fresh, spiced rice wine. The West Lake of Hangzhou gave the ancient city fine, freshwater fish as well as natural beauty. Some of the fine results include West Lake vinegar fish, and West Lake watercress is a connoisseur's delight. The tea-houses by the lake were famed for their service of another Hangzhou speciality, Dragon Well Tea (*Loong Ching*). The tea is China's finest, a delicate, slightly bitter green tea, as rare and special as good champagne and still used for special state occasions.

OUTSIDE SHANGHAI, China's largest city, the scenery and way of life of the Yangtze delta remain unchanged.

Hangzhou has other claims to fame. Hangzhou dumplings are gloriously filled with meat and sauce. Quick-fried shredded eel, often regarded as a Shanghainese delicacy, actually originated in Hangzhou, as did the beggar's chicken, mentioned in the introduction to Peking cuisine, which happily adopted a Hangzhou peasant thief's invention!

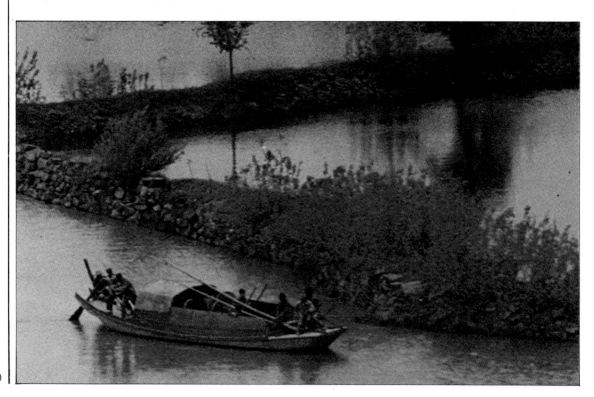

Suzhou was another Sung dynasty city of grace and beauty. An old Chinese saying claimed that 'Above is paradise; here below are Suzhou and Hangzhou'. Another watery wonderland of bridges and streams, Suzhou attracted poets and gourmets.

Favorite Suzhou recipes are Chinese ham in honey sauce and winter bamboo shoots with shrimp eggs (salty preserved goodness reappearing in fine forms). Suzhou is also associated with the freshwater crabs, known to the world as Shanghai crabs. Every autumn the crabs emerge from the Yangtze River mudlands, their mating urges driving them on to dry land and into fishermen's traps. Millions of them find themselves trussed up in green grass thongs, packed in ice and shipped off as a major export from Shanghai.

Shaohsing wine, a product of the fertile river valley, is a rice spirit that appears in many Chinese dishes. Other products of the area include Zhenjiang's vinegar and Amoy's soy sauce.

One authority believes that some of China's best vegetarian dishes are found in the Shanghai school of cooking. Such dishes are made by both Taoist and Buddhist chefs: Buddhists do not eat meat from religious conviction while Taoists have long studied the correct use of vegetables for long life and good health.

Away from the monasteries other meat dishes were being pioneered in the Shanghai region. Thus Nanking, a former capital during troubled times, has given us fine pressed duck, and Wuxi exported the idea and brilliance of sweet-and-sour pork spare ribs. Sizzling rice dishes come from the eastern region, from Yangzhou, which was also the home of the banquet-ending rice and noodles with vegetables.

The cuisine of Fukien Province bears a closer relationship to the cooking traditions of its neighbours to the south, Chiu Chow and Guangzhou. Amoy and Fuzhou are the province's major ports, facing the Taiwan Strait, and in the past centuries, thousands of Fukienese emigrated from such ports to take their diverse culinary ideas to the Philippines, Singapore and elsewhere.

One Shanghainese element in their cooking is the frequent use of the 'red cooking' technique, a slow stewing or braising of soy-sauced dishes, in which the reduction of cooking oils produces hot tastiness. Unless the dish is eaten quickly, the greasiness for which Shanghainese food is notorious emerges.

Generally meticulously chopped or shredded, Fukienese food is of a soft consistency and soups are favorites. Congee, which a westerner might call rice porridge, is a Fukienese speciality, but most of the province's dishes are plain and simple and many of them employ the southern technique of stir-frying.

With all the variety of Shanghainese cooking it's not surprising that a typical overseas Shanghainese café menu can be both massive and baffling. It will have Sichuan and Cantonese dishes, along with dishes favored by the seagoing Hoklo or farming Hakka peoples. For Shanghai was a cultural melting pot for a century and also renowned for its 'Russian' bakeries. It was also a region of convivial, gregarious diners who did not stand on ceremony. They were snackers rather than banqueteers, for Shanghai was the city of business while Peking was the seat of government. Shanghai was exciting. It was a city for all seasons and its Shanghainese cooking proves it.

A SUMMER HOUSE on Hangzhou's West Lake.

清炒蝦仁

STIR-FRIED SHRIMP WITH GREEN PEAS

苑碗荳蝦仁

STIR-FRIED SHRIMP WITH GREEN PEAS
This dish can be prepared almost in an instant by stir-frying. Indeed, the shortness of the cooking time is a key factor in the quality of the result: a crisp outer shell with a fresh, juicy morsel within. Biting into the shrimp should feel exactly like biting into an apple.

STIR-FRIED BROAD BEANS, SHRIMP, HAM AND BUTTON MUSHROOMS
In this semi-soup dish the flavor of the beans is set off against the savoriness of the shrimp and the richly flavored sauce.

清
炒
蝦
仁

STIR-FRIED SHRIMP WITH GREEN PEAS

1¼lb shrimp, shelled and deveined	1 tsp sesame oil
	2 cups peanut oil
	2 slices fresh ginger
Marinade	9oz green peas
1 egg white	2 tbsp chicken stock
2 tsp cornstarch	½ tsp salt
1 tsp salt	1 tsp Chinese yellow wine

Clean the shrimp and pat them dry. Mix together the marinade ingredients, add the shrimp and refrigerate for 30 minutes.

Heat 2 tbsp oil in a pan. Add the ginger but remove and discard it when it has browned. Add the green peas to the pan and the stock and ½ tsp salt. Cook for 2 minutes, remove, drain and set aside. Heat 2 cups oil in the pan and add the shrimp, stirring to separate. Remove.

Reheat the pan, return the shrimp and green peas and add the Chinese yellow wine. Stir rapidly over a very high heat for 30 seconds and serve.

STIR-FRIED SHRIMP

1¼lb shelled shrimp, fresh or frozen	**Seasonings**
	1½ tsp chopped fresh ginger
1 egg white	2 tsp chopped scallion
2 tsp cornstarch	2 tsp Chinese yellow wine
2 cups peanut oil	few drops vinegar
	1 tsp salt

Clean the shrimp and dry them with a paper towel. Blend the egg white and cornstarch and coat the shrimp with the mixture.

Bring the oil to the boil. Add the shrimp, stirring to separate. After 30 seconds remove the shrimp from the pan quickly and drain them thoroughly.

Heat the pan until it is very hot and add 1 tbsp peanut oil. Add the seasonings and then the shrimp. Stir rapidly for 20 seconds over a high heat.

STIR-FRIED BROAD BEANS, SHRIMP, HAM AND BUTTON MUSHROOMS

1¼lb broad beans	1 tsp cornstarch
	1 tsp salt
Marinade	¼ tsp sesame oil
½ egg white	

8oz shrimp, shelled and deveined

4oz ham
4oz button mushrooms
1 cup peanut oil

3—4 slices fresh ginger
2 cloves garlic, crushed
1 cup chicken stock
2 tsp Chinese yellow wine
2 tbsp cornstarch
1 tsp sugar
1 tsp salt

Skin the beans and top-and-tail them. Set aside.

Prepare the marinade. Clean the shrimp, pat them dry and set them aside to marinate.

Cut the ham into $\frac{1}{8}$in thin slices, then cut it into $\frac{1}{2}$in squares. Set aside.

Cut the mushrooms horizontally in halves. Set aside.

Heat the oil. When it is hot add the shrimp, stirring to separate. After 30 seconds remove and drain. Set aside.

Fry the beans and button mushrooms in the oil for $1\frac{1}{2}$ minutes over a high heat. Remove, drain and set aside.

Heat 3 tbsp oil in the pan. Add the ginger slices and crushed garlic and remove and discard them when browned.

Return the shrimp to the pan. Sauté for 30 seconds, stir and add the broad beans, ham and mushrooms. Add the remaining ingredients, stir and bring to the boil quickly. Continue to stir-fry over high heat for $1\frac{1}{2}$ minutes and serve.

SHANGHAI QUICK-FRY SHRIMP

12oz fresh shrimp, shelled
1 egg white
2 tsp cornstarch
2 cups peanut oil

Seasonings
$1\frac{1}{2}$ tsp chopped fresh ginger

$1\frac{1}{2}$ tsp chopped scallion
$1\frac{1}{2}$ tsp rice wine
2 drops white vinegar
1 tsp monosodium glutamate
   (optional)
$\frac{1}{2}$ tsp of salt

Clean the shrimp and dry them with a towel.

Mix together the egg white and cornstarch and use the mixture to coat the shrimp.

Bring the oil to a high temperature in a pan.

Add the shrimp, stir to separate and fry for 15 seconds. Remove the shrimp from the pan with a perforated spoon and drain away the oil.

Heat a pan or wok until it is very hot. Pour 1 tbsp peanut oil into it and add the seasonings and the shrimp. Fry for 20 seconds over a high heat and serve.

The success of this dish relies very much on temperature — it needs very high heat and quick stir-frying.

清蒸河鰻

STEAMED EEL and
(*below*) SIZZLING EEL
Eel is a favorite dish all
along the Yangtze River.
In Shanghai, along the
lower reaches of this great
waterway, the eel flesh is
often steamed and
presented more delicately
than in Sichuan and the
upper Yangtze. There the
sauce used is much more
spicy: the eel is first fried,
then cut into strips to be
given a turn in a highly
spiced sauce (see picture
below). The Shanghai
version is excellent with
wine: the overpowering
flavor of the Sichuan
version is best with
quantities of rice.

炒蟮糊

WEST LAKE FISH
Most of the larger Chinese cities, including Shanghai, have a West Lake — a place where the townsfolk can relax and entertain themselves. The title of this dish denotes the proximity of the water in which the fish (usually carp) was caught — and thus the freshness of the fish. This is a deep-fried version which may be presented with either a savory or sweet-and-sour sauce, the total flavor made more distinctive by sprinkling the dish with chopped coriander.

清蒸河鰻

STEAMED EEL

2lb white eel	*1 cup chicken stock*
6 slices fresh ginger	*1 tsp salt*
2 scallions	*1 tsp sugar*
8 tbsp peanut oil	*½ tsp pepper*
1 tsp Chinese yellow wine	*1 tbsp cornstarch*

Put the eel in a bowl and pour over it 10 cups boiling water with 2 tbsp salt added. Wash the fish thoroughly. Slit the eel open, remove the intestines and clean the inside carefully. Pat it dry with paper towels.

Make deep cuts (about three-quarters of the way through the flesh) at 1in intervals along the eel and place it on a plate, bending it into a ring form. Arrange the ginger and scallions on top.

Steam the eel over a medium heat for 20 minutes. Remove the ginger and scallions and discard them and drain away the liquid from the plate. Heat the oil and pour it over the eel, again draining any excess from the plate.

Add the remaining ingredients to the pan, stir and bring to the boil. Pour the sauce over the eel and serve.

SIZZLING EEL

2lb yellow eels	*2 tbsp dark soy sauce*
10 cups boiling water	*¼ cup chicken stock*
2 tbsp salt	*1½ tbsp cornstarch dissolved in*
4 tbsp peanut oil	*water*
2 tsp chopped ginger	*2 tsp chopped scallions*
½ tsp pepper	*2 tbsp sesame oil*
2 tsp Chinese yellow wine	*2 tsp minced ham*
1 tbsp sugar	*1½ tsp chopped coriander*
	(cilantro)

Place the eels in a bowl. Pour over them the boiling water (to which has been added 2 tbsp salt) and let them stand for 3 minutes. Take the eels out of the water and rinse them in cold water from the tap.

Separate the meat from the bone with the handle of a tea-spoon, then cut the eel meat into ½ × 2in strips. Set aside. Heat the oil until very hot. Add the eel, stirring, and add the chopped ginger, pepper, yellow wine, sugar, soy sauce and chicken stock. Cook for 5 minutes. Stir in the cornstarch and transfer to a plate. Make a small well in the center of the eels and put into it the chopped scallion.

Heat 2 tbsp sesame oil until very hot and pour it into the 'well'. Add the minced ham, garnish with coriander and serve.

西
湖
醋
魚

WEST LAKE FISH

2lb carp	**Sauce**
2 tbsp shredded ginger	*1 cup chicken stock*
3 tbsp shredded scallion	*1 tbsp sugar*
generous ½ cup peanut oil	*1 tbsp brown vinegar*
	1 tsp salt
	¼ tsp pepper
	1½ tbsp cornstarch
	2 tsp Chinese yellow wine

Put the fish in a basin. Pour over it 5 cups boiling water and leave it to stand for 1 minute.

Scrape off the scales and place the fish on a chopping-board. Slicing horizontally, cut the fish in two, one side with the back bone, the other without. On the side with the back bone, make five deep slits, approximately 1½in apart.

On the meat side of the other half make a long lengthwise slit, but do not cut through the skin.

Place the whole fish, including the head, on a plate. Spread the ginger and half the scallion over it and steam over a high heat for 10 minutes. Remove and discard the scallion and arrange the remaining fresh scallion on top of the fish. Heat ¼ cup peanut oil in a pan and pour it over the fish, draining away any excess from the plate.

Heat 2 tbsp oil in a pan and add the sauce ingredients. Bring the sauce to the boil, pour it over the fish and serve.

CHICKEN 'SAUCE'

1½lb young chicken	*8 tbsp stock*
2 tbsp lard	*1 tbsp cornstarch*
1½ tbsp rice wine or dry sherry	*2 scallions, cut into 1in lengths*
2 tbsp soy sauce	
1 tbsp sugar	

Cut off the wings and parson's nose of the chicken, then chop it into about 20 pieces with the bone still attached.

Heat up the lard over a high heat; stir-fry the chicken pieces for about 30 seconds.

Add wine or sherry, soy sauce and sugar; stir until the chicken turns brown then add the stock. Bring it to the boil, reduce heat to simmer for 10 minutes or until the stock is reduced by approximately one-third.

Increase the heat, add the cornstarch mixed in a little water,

醉
雞

DRUNKEN CHICKEN

DRUNKEN CHICKEN

Served principally as a
cold *hors d'oeuvre*, the
chicken is lightly boiled,
then immersed in wine for
a period which may be a
few hours or a few days.
The chicken used should
be a free-range fowl for
choice: if not, the chicken
should be marinated
overnight to improve its
flavor.

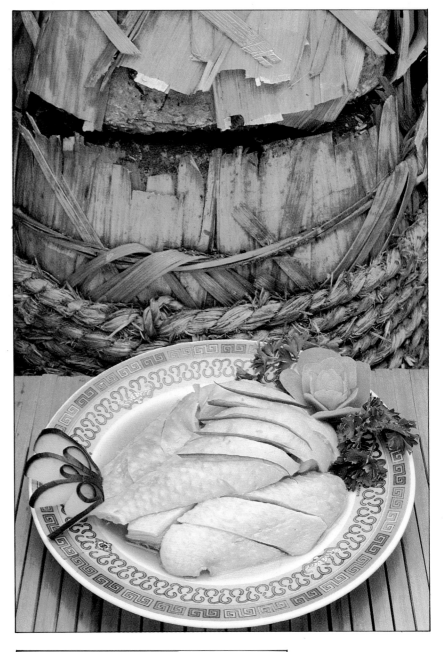

BEGGAR'S CHICKEN

This amusing barbecue
dish should be cooked for
several hours in the
embers of a hot fire. The
chicken, well marinated, is
wrapped in lotus leaves
than plastered with mud.
The name of the dish
indicates the Chinese
admiration for the
resourcefulness of the
poor man — and suggests
that the recipe should
begin 'First steal one
chicken'.

醬
爆
櫻
桃

HONEY HAM
The Chinese often use honey, sugar or syrup to cook or flavor salty meat. This is a typical example, in which the saltiness of the ham contrasts interestingly with the sweetness of the honey sauce.

STIR-FRIED FROGS' LEGS IN BROWN SAUCE
In Chinese cuisine, frog is treated like chicken, with the advantage that frog can be cooked in even less time than chicken. This is really a reproduction chicken dish in which the frog is cooked very quickly in a brown soy-paste sauce. The fresh savoriness of the frog is contrasted with the earthier savor of the brown sauce: the dish can be made more aromatic by the last-minute addition of some wine.

blend well. When the juice is further reduced by half add the scallions and serve.

Each chicken piece should be wrapped in a dark, thickish sauce, hence the name of this dish.

DRUNKEN CHICKEN

2lb chicken	*4oz fresh ginger*
1 tbsp salt	*1 cup Chinese yellow wine*
2 scallions	

Clean the chicken thoroughly. Bring 10 cups water to the boil, turn off the heat, place the chicken in the hot water and turn it over. Poach the chicken for 1 minute, remove, drain and pat it dry with an absorbent paper towel.

Rub ½ tbsp salt over the skin and spoon ½ tbsp salt into the cavity. Finely shred the scallion and ginger and stuff them into the cavity. Finally, pour the Chinese yellow wine into the cavity.

Steam the chicken over medium heat for 20 minutes in a shallow basin. Remove it and chop it into bite-size pieces. Return the chicken pieces to the wine in the basin, soak overnight and transfer to a plate to serve.

HONEY HAM

12oz Chinese ham	*2 tbsp peanut oil*
11oz candied lotus seeds	*1 tsp dried laurel blossoms*
½ cup sugar	*(Cointreau is a good substitute)*

Clean the ham thoroughly with hot water before placing it in a deep container. Add sufficient water to cover and steam for 2 hours. Remove and drain.

Place the candied lotus seeds in a separate container and add 1 cup water. Steam for 2 hours and set aside.

Cut the ham into slices 1 × 2½ × ⅛in and arrange them neatly in a medium-size bowl. Add water to cover the ham and steam for 30 minutes. Drain, sprinkle with sugar and steam for another 30 minutes.

Arrange the ham slices carefully on top of the lotus seeds and steam for 10 minutes.

Heat 2 tbsp oil in a pan and add the gravy from the ham. Add the dried laurel blossoms, stirring over a low heat for 1 minute. Pour the sweet gravy over the ham and serve.

醬爆櫻桃

STIR-FRIED FROGS' LEGS IN BROWN SAUCE

3 tbsp peanut oil
6 scallions (white part only)
2 tsp chopped fresh ginger
24 pieces frogs' legs
1 tbsp Chinese yellow wine

1 tsp sugar
1 tbsp dark soy sauce
4 tbsp chicken stock
½ tsp five-spice powder
1 tsp sesame oil

Heat 3 tbsp oil in a pan. Add the scallions and ginger and when the aroma arises, add the frogs' legs. Stirring, cook over a very high heat for 30 seconds.

Add the yellow wine, sugar, dark soy sauce and chicken stock and, when they boil, reduce the heat and cook until the sauce has almost evaporated.

Sprinkle with five-spice powder and sesame oil, stir and serve.

BEGGAR'S CHICKEN

Marinade
2 tbsp dark soy sauce
4 tbsp Chinese yellow wine
1 tsp sesame oil
1 tsp sugar
1 tbsp salt

3-4lb chicken

Stuffing
4-6 Chinese black mushrooms

1¼lb pork
4oz Sichuan preserved vegetables
14oz bamboo shoots
2 tbsp peanut oil

1 large piece suet
2 pieces lotus leaf
1¼lb all-purpose flour
2 cups water
1 large piece foil

Blend together the ingredients for the marinade and use three-quarters of the mixture to rub over the inside and outside of the chicken. Set aside.

Prepare the stuffing by soaking the black mushrooms in hot water for 30 minutes. Discard the stems and shred the caps.

Shred the pork and mix it with the remaining quarter of the marinade.

Shred the Sichuan preserved vegetables into matchstick-size pieces and soak them in water.

Shred the bamboo shoots into similar pieces and blanch them in boiling water for 2 minutes. (When using canned bamboo shoots this is not necessary.)

Heat a pan, add 2 tbsp peanut oil and stir-fry the pork for 1 minute.

Add the shredded black mushrooms, bamboo shoots and Sichuan preserved vegetables. Cook for 30 seconds and stuff the

韭
黄
炒
肉
絲

DRY-BRAISED BAMBOO SHOOTS

DRY-BRAISED BAMBOO SHOOTS
WITH PRESERVED SNOW
CABBAGE
This is a dish for the
connoisseur because the
flavor of the fresh
bamboo shoot is
extremely subtle. Here it
is set off by a typical east
Chinese pickle which is
extremely salty. The dish
is often served as a hot
hors d'oeuvre for diners
to nibble at while they sip
their wine.

STIR-FRIED SHREDDED PORK
AND CHINESE WHITE CHIVES
This may be readily
produced in a very short
time, either as a hot *hors
d'oeuvre* to accompany
wine or to be added to
rice to increase the
savoriness of the whole
meal. Chinese chives are
not widely available but
are worth searching for.

STIR-FRIED SHREDDED BEEF
AND GREEN PEPPER
A lower Yangtze dish
which approximates to a
Sichuan (upper Yangtze)
dish of rather similar
composition. In the
version illustrated here,
chili pepper has been
added to the stir-fry along
with the sweet pepper,
lending a spicy
savoriness to the dish.
Delicious with rice.

214

青椒牛肉絲

mixture generously into the cavity of the chicken.

Wrap the chicken in the piece of suet, trimming away any excess fat, and wrap the suet and chicken parcel in lotus leaves. (If you are using dried lotus leaves, soak them in hot water for 10 minutes first.)

Mix the flour and water and roll it out into a sheet. Encase the chicken parcel in the dough and wrap it all with foil.

Cook in a pre-heated oven at 450°F for 1 hour. Reduce the temperature to 350°F and bake for a further 45 minutes.

Remove the foil and crack the dough casing with a pestle. Carefully remove the lotus leaves and transfer the chicken to a serving platter.

STIR-FRIED SHREDDED BEEF AND GREEN PEPPER

12oz fillet of beef	*1 egg white*
Marinade	*1¼lb green pepper*
1 tbsp light soy sauce	*1 cup peanut oil*
1 tsp dark soy sauce	*1 tsp salt*
1 tsp sugar	*2 tsp chopped fresh ginger*
1 tbsp cornstarch	*2 tsp choppd garlic*
2 tbsp Chinese yellow wine	*2 tsp Chinese yellow wine*

Shred the beef and mix the pieces thoroughly with the marinade mixture in a bowl. Allow to stand for 15 minutes.

Shred the green pepper.

Heat the oil in a pan and add the beef, stirring to separate the shreds. Remove after 75 seconds, drain and set aside.

Heat 1 tbsp oil in the pan, add the green pepper and 1 tsp of salt, stir-frying for 2 minutes over high heat. Remove and set aside.

Heat 2 tbsp oil in the pan. Add the ginger and garlic and, when the aroma arises, return the beef and green pepper to the pan. Add any of the marinade mixture that is left in the bowl and stir-fry over very high heat for 2½ minutes. Add Chinese yellow wine and serve.

STIR-FRIED SHREDDED PORK AND CHINESE WHITE CHIVES

500g (1¼l of pork	*1 egg white*
1¼lb fillet	*1 tbsp cornstarch*
Marinade	*2 tsp Chinese yellow wine or dry*
1 tbsp light soy sauce	*sherry*
½ tsp sesame oil	

韭
黄
炒
肉
絲

2 medium black mushrooms
8oz Chinese white chives or young
   leeks
1 cup peanut oil
1½ tsp chopped fresh ginger

1 tsp chopped garlic
1 tsp salt
1 tsp Chinese yellow wine or dry
   sherry

Cut the fillet of pork into ⅛in thin slices. Then into 2in shreds. Mix the pieces of meat with the marinade and set them aside for 15 minutes.

Soak the black mushrooms in hot water for 30 minutes. Remove and discard the stems and cup the caps into fine shreds. Cut the chives or leeks into shreds 2in long.

Heat 1 cup peanut oil in pan. Add the pork, stirring to separate, reduce the heat, and leave to sit in the oil for 2 minutes. Remove, drain and set aside.

Heat 2 tbsp oil in a pan. Add the ginger and garlic, return the pork and add the mushrooms, chives or leeks and salt. Stir and cook over high heat for 2 minutes, add the Chinese yellow wine, stir again and serve.

DRY-BRAISED BAMBOO SHOOTS WITH PRESERVED SNOW CABBAGE

8oz bamboo shoot
6oz preserved snow cabbage
4-6 stalks scallions (white part
   only)
4 tbsp peanut oil

3-4 slices fresh ginger
1 tsp salt
1 tbsp sugar
2 tbsp Chinese yellow wine
4 tbsp chicken stock

Cut the bamboo shoot into wedges ¾in long.

Soak the preserved snow cabbage in 5 cups cold water for 30 minutes. Change the water and soak for a further 15 minutes. Chop into sections 1½in long. Cut the scallions into sections the same length.

Heat 2 tbsp oil in a pan and add the scallions and ginger. When the aroma arises, add the bamboo shoot and snow cabbage and stir-fry over a high heat for 2 minutes.

Add the remaining ingredients and continue to stir-fry and cook over a very high heat for 3 minutes. Remove from the heat and drain away any remaining liquid.

Heat 2 tbsp oil in the pan until very hot. Return the drained bamboo shoot and snow cabbage to fry for a further 2 minutes. Remove and drain again on a paper towel before transferring to the serving dish.

GLOSSARY

Bamboo shoots: There are several kinds of bamboo shoots available in the West — all in cans only, which is a pity since they lose much of their crispy texture and flavor. Try to obtain *Winter bamboo shoots*; they are dug up from the cracked earth before the shoots grow to any great length or size and are therefore extra tender and tasty. Spring bamboo shoots are much larger; they sometimes may reach several feet in length and 3-4in in diameter. Once the can is opened, the shoots may be kept in a covered jar of water in the refrigerator for several days. *Braised bamboo shoots* in cans should be eaten cold without any further cooking.

Bean curd (tofu): Made from soaked yellow soy beans ground with water. A coagulant is added after some of the water is strained through muslin cloth, causing the ground beans to curdle and become firm bean curd. Usually sold in squares about $2\frac{1}{2}\times2\frac{1}{2}$in and $\frac{3}{4}$in thick, it will keep a few days if submerged in water in a container and placed in the coldest part of a refrigerator. *Dried bean curd skin* is usually sold either in thick sticks or thin sheets. It should be soaked in cold water overnight or in warm water for at least an hour before use.

Bean sauce: Sometimes called 'Crushed bean sauce', this thick sauce is made from black or yellow beans, flour and salt. It is sold in cans and, once opened, must be transferred into a screw-top jar and then it will keep in a refrigerator for months. (N.B. Black bean sauce is very salty, while yellow bean sauce is sweeter with sugar added.)

Bean sprouts: Two kinds are available: *yellow soy bean sprouts*, only to be found in Chinese provision stores, and *green mung bean sprouts*, which can be bought from almost every large city supermarket. (Never use canned bean sprouts, they do not have the crunchy texture which is the main characteristic of bean sprouts.) They can be kept in the refrigerator for two or three days if bought fresh.

Cellophane or transparent noodles: Made from mung beans. They are sold in dried form, tied into bundles weighing from 2oz to 1lb. Soak in warm water for 5 minutes before use.

Chili paste: Also called 'Chili purée'. Is made of chilli, soybean, salt, sugar and flour. Sold in jars, it will keep almost indefinitely.

Chili sauce: Hot, red sauce made from chilies, vinegar, plums, salt and sesame.

Chinese cabbage: There are innumerable varieties of cabbage grown in China, of which only two or three types are available in the West. The one most commonly seen is known as celery cabbage or Chinese leaves (*Brassica pekinensis*), it has a pale green color and tightly wrapped elongated head; two-thirds of the vegetable is stem which has a crunchy texture. Another variety has a shorter and fatter head with curlier, pale yellow leaves. Then there is the dark green-leaved variety, also with white stems (*Brassica chinensis*), and the bright green-leaved variety with pale green stems, sometimes with a sprig of yellow flower in the center (*Brassica parachinensis*) which is very much prized by the Chinese. These last two varieties are sold only in Chinese stores.

Chinese dried mushrooms: There are two main types of Chinese mushrooms: those that grow on trees, known as Black or Winter Mushrooms (*Lentinus edodes*); and those cultivated on a bed of straw, known as Straw Mushrooms (*Volvariella volvacea*). Black or Winter Mushrooms are sold dried; they are used in many dishes as a complementary vegetable for their flavor and aroma. Soak in warm water for 20-30 minutes, squeeze dry and discard the hard stalks before use. Straw Mushrooms are available in cans and are completely different in texture and flavor. The Western varieties of common or field mushrooms (*Agaricus bisporus* or *Psalliota campestris*) can be used as substitutes.

Five-spice powder: A mixture of anise seed, fennel, cloves, cinnamon and pepper. It is very strongly piquant, so use a very small amount each time. It will keep for years if stored in a tightly covered container.

Fresh coriander: Sometimes known as Chinese parsley, this plant is available in Oriental stores, or in Italian grocers where it is called *cilantro*.

Ginger root: Sold by weight. Should be peeled and sliced or finely chopped before use. Will keep for weeks in a dry, cool place. Dried and powdered ginger is not a satisfactory substitute for fresh ginger.

Green hot chili: Will keep fresh for a week or two in the vegetable compartment of the refrigerator in a plastic bag.

Hoisin sauce: Also known as barbecue sauce. Made from soybeans, sugar, flour, vinegar, salt, garlic, chili and sesame.

Monosodium glutamate (MSG): This chemical is an optional addition in Chinese cooking. Sometime known as 'taste essence' (*veh t'sin*), it is often used to heighten the flavor of food. It is rather frowned upon by true gourmets as it can wipe out the subtle flavors of a dish when used to excess, so use with discretion.

Oyster sauce: A thick sauce made from oysters and soysauce. Sold in bottles, it will keep in the refrigerator indefinitely.

Red bean curd sauce: A thick sauce made from fermented bean curd and salt. Sold in cans or jars, it will keep indefinitely.

Rice wine: Also known as Shaohsing wine, made from glutinous rice. Saké or pale (medium or dry) sherry can be substituted.

Salted black beans: Whole bean sauce, very salty.

Scallions: A long-necked onion without a normal bulb.

Sesame seed oil: Sold in bottles. Widely used in China as a garnish rather than for cooking. The refined yellow sesame oil sold in Middle Eastern stores has less flavor and therefore is not a very satisfactory substitute.

A few words must be said here regarding the types of oil used in Chinese cooking. The most commonly used in China are vegetable oils such as soybean, peanut or rape seed oils. The Chinese never use butter or meat dripping, although lard and chicken fat are used in some regional cooking, notably in the Eastern School.

Sichuan preserved vegetable: This is a speciality of Sichuan province. It is the root of a special variety of the mustard green, pickled in salt and hot chili. Sold in cans. Once opened it can be stored in a tightly sealed jar in the refrigerator for months.

Sichuan peppercorns: Reddish-brown peppercorns, much stronger than either black or white peppercorns of the West. Usually sold in plastic bags. Will keep indefinitely in a tightly sealed container.

Soysauce: Sold in bottles or cans, this liquid sauce ranges from light to dark brown in color. The darker colored sauces are strongest and more often used in cooking, whereas the lighter are used at the table.

Tiger lily or **golden needles:** The buds of a special type of lily (*Hemerocallis fulva*). Sold in dried form, they should be soaked in warm water for 10-20 minutes and the hard stems removed. They are often used in combination with *Wood-ears*.

Tomato sauce: Quite different from Western tomato ketchup. Italian tomato paste (purée) may be substituted when fresh tomatoes are not available.

Water chestnuts: Strictly speaking, water chestnuts do not belong to the chestnut family, they are the roots of a vegetable (*Heleocharis tuberosa*). Also known as *horse's hooves* in China on account of their appearance before the skin is peeled off, they are available fresh or in cans. Canned water chestnuts retain only part of the texture, and even less of the flavor, of fresh ones. Will keep for about a month in a refrigerator in a covered jar.

Water chestnut powder: A flour made from water chestnuts. Cornstarch is a good substitute.

Wood-ears: Also known as *Cloud Ears*, they are dried tree fungus (*Auricularia auricula*). Sold in dried form, they should be soaked in warm water for 20 minutes; discard any hard stems and rinse in fresh water before use. They have a crunchy texture and a mild but subtle flavor. According to the Chinese, Wood-ears contain protein, calcium, phosphorus, iron and carbohydrates, and one particular brand from Hupei Province claims on the packet (in English) that it 'possesses such effect as cleaning gastroenteric (sic!) organs in human body'.

INDEX

Page numbers in *italic* refer
to the illustrations.

221

222